APPEL IS FOREVER

APPEL IS FOREVER

A Child's Memoir

Suzanne Mehler Whiteley

 Wayne State University Press   Detroit

03 02 01 00 99   5 4 3 2 1

Library of Congress Cataloging-in-Publication Data

Whiteley, Suzanne Mehler, 1935–
    Appel is forever ; a child's memoir / Suzanne Mehler Whiteley.
        p.   cm.
    Includes bibliographical references.
    Summary: The author describes her experiences during the Holocaust
between the ages of five and nine, in Amsterdam, as a prisoner in the
Westerbork and Bergen-Belsen concentration camps, and eventually in the
United States.
    ISBN 0-8143-2821-0 (alk. paper). — ISBN 0-8143-2822-9 (pbk. : alk.
paper)
    1. Whiteley, Suzanne Mehler, 1935–   . —Juvenile literature. 2. Jewish
children—Netherlands—Amsterdam—Biography—Juvenile literature.
3. Jewish children in the Holocaust—Germany—Biography—Juvenile literature. 4. Bergen-Belsen (Concentration camp)—Juvenile literature.
5. Westerbork (Concentration camp)—Juvenile literature. 6. Holocaust,
Jewish (1939–1945)—Personal narratives—Juvenile literature. 7. Holocaust
survivors—United States—Biography—Juvenile literature. [1. Whiteley,
Suzanne Mehler, 1935–   . 2. Jews—Netherlands—Biography.
3. Holocaust, Jewish (1939–1945)—Personal narratives. 4. Westerbork
(Netherlands : Concentration camp) 5. Bergen-Belsen (Germany :
Concentration camp) 6. Women—Biography.]   I. Title
DS135.N6W54   1999
940.53'18'09492352—dc21   98-55432

In memory of
Elsa Glaserfeld, beloved Oma, murdered in Auschwitz
Ludwig Jacob Mehler, my father, murdered in Bergen-Belsen
Catherine K. Cullinan, M.D., who gave me back my life and who said,
"The hardest part of your therapy was having to relive your childhood with you."

For
Margaret Glaserfeld Mehler, my mother, who used all her courage and then some
and
The children, M, M, A, S, and R, and for all those who come after them

And in memory of Antoon and Truus Evers
whose sons brought vegetables to my family during the occupation
who nursed my mother and gave her hope
whose friendship continues now across an ocean
between Wilfred and Nel Evers and Suzanne Mehler Whiteley

CONTENTS

Part 3

PREFACE

One morning in the spring of 1989, I popped awake, sat upright in my bed, and heard myself say, "You have to do this and you have to do it now; you cannot wait any longer!"

"It" was the writing of a memoir that would describe my experiences as a child of five, six, seven, eight, and nine during World War II. Since the age of thirteen, I had thought to write down my war experiences but I was never able to do it. Over the years, I found many reasons not to: "Who needs another war story?" or "I can't write" or "It will never convey what it was really like—it won't even come close!"

But other impulses drove me. Initially, I wanted to write this for my children. I had never been able to talk about the Holocaust with them. Then I thought of my close friends and discovered I believe no one "knows" me who doesn't know the life I lived as a little girl. And how much, how much we want to be "known" to those who are important to us!

We also need to be "known" to ourselves. I could not have imagined the effect writing these memories would have on me. For the first time I realized that these are the conscious memories. What happened on the many days I do not consciously remember? For the first time I realized that I was once a small child. I never thought of myself as a child. When I look at children who are six, seven, eight, and nine years old I am always shocked to see how small they are.

Finally, I wanted to make this material accessible to those young and older people who have no knowledge of what happened in Europe just a few decades ago.

I didn't know what I was getting into. As I worked I wrote about much more than the two years in the camps. But when I finished writing I felt myself to be a different person. I cannot explain this even to myself but there is a "before" and an "after" self. I am calmer, more confident, and more at home in this world.

I deliberately stopped the narrative at the point of attaining adulthood. Establishing a woman's adult life is another story entirely. Neither did I write in detail about the lifelong emotional and physical aftermath of my war experiences. My judgment is that such material does not belong in a child's memoir.

ACKNOWLEDGMENTS

Throughout the writing of this memoir, dear friends encouraged me. My heart glows when I think of Emily and Dick Axelrod, Jackie Granat, Barbara Stock Kozel, Joyce Lopas, and David Koenig.

A separate and heartfelt acknowledgment goes to Winifred Wanderwalker Farbman. From the start she entered my words into her computer and page by page gave me unbelievable feedback. She enabled me to continue writing. Thank you is not enough, but I say, "Thank you, Winifred."

Irvin and Joan Noparstak were a serendipitous gift from heaven. This serendipity connected me with Elizabeth Reis, professor of modern history at the University of Oregon in Eugene. Her special excitement and very hard work encouraged me to finish this manuscript. With sensitivity and great perseverance, she helped see this project through to publication. I will always think of her with appreciation and gratitude.

TIME AND GEOGRAPHICAL SEQUENCE

1934–43   Amsterdam, Holland

1943   Westerbork, a transit camp in Holland

1943–45   Bergen-Belsen, a concentration camp in northern Germany

1945   Troibitz, a village in northeastern Germany in the Russian zone of occupation

1945   Leipzig, city in East Germany

1945   Maastricht, city in southern tip of Netherlands

1945   Amsterdam, Holland

1945–46   Copenhagen, Denmark

1946–47   Amsterdam, Holland

1947   New York, USA

1947–   Chicago, USA

INTRODUCTION

In the 1930s many German Jewish families fled Germany and came to hospitable Holland. Holland had been neutral in World War I and people hoped it could be neutral again in the impending war. Amsterdam had a sizable refugee community and many of the German Jewish families joined the large Liberal Jewish Synagogue of Amsterdam. Holland also had a more established orthodox population which periodically was enlarged by Jewish families fleeing the various disasters of Eastern Europe. The longest established Jewish population was made up of the descendents of the Sephardic Jews. These made their home in Holland in the years after the 1492 expulsion from Spain. In 1492 Queen Isabella and King Ferdinand finished their "ethnic cleansing" of Spain by throwing out the remaining Muslim Moors and all the Jews who would not convert to Catholicism.

Holland has a tradition of tolerance. Perhaps the age-old communal struggle to hold the land against the always threatening sea created a different mindset than that of other European lands. Holland's long fight in the 1500s for independence from autocratic, imperial Spain must have been influential in forming the national character. After the Spanish were defeated Holland had to accommodate itself to being half Catholic (in the south) and half Protestant (in the north). During the long years of religious absolutism this ability to live peaceably together in the same national entity must have required some ability to tolerate "differences."

Holland's own "golden age" of accomplishment and imperialism set it on a unique path that furthered a distinct Dutch culture. When Rembrandt painted he used his Jewish neighbors as models for some of

13

his biblical paintings. When Napoleon was triumphant after the French Revolution of 1789 his army occupied Holland and he put his brother on the Dutch throne in 1806. He also spread the egalitarian ideas of the French Revolution. In the early 1800s emancipation came to many of the European countries. It meant that Jewish people could now be citizens of the lands they lived in and were required to take a last name, that is, a family name.

Holland's openness to foreigners such as Huguenots, English pilgrims, and Jews was not its only characteristic. A strongly conservative streak coexisted, as shown by some of the rigidities of the early Dutch Reform's strict Protestantism, of the well-defined class system, and of the behaviors of some of the expatriate Dutch colonizers. In the years following World War I and the Great Depression, Holland, too, had its homegrown fascists. This nazi party was known by the acronym of NSB.

In September 1939, Germany attacked Poland and Blitzkrieg became a new reality. In May 1940, Germany attacked the Netherlands and Belgium. It was easy to "blitz" across the borders. The land was flat, cultivated farmland with good roads. The Dutch army fought five days before surrendering to the Germans. Concurrently the port city of Rotterdam had its center bombed out of existence. The Dutch queen, Wilhelmina, and her family and household fled to England and then to Canada, where they remained until the end of World War II.

The occupation lasted five long years. Hitler's original intent was to use propaganda to nazify the population as fellow "Aryans" and eventually annex the country as part of the greater Reich. From May 1940 to spring 1941 the Germans behaved relatively mildly in Holland. Then German policies became more demanding and punitive: rationing, labor callups to work in Germany, and the implementation of the legal structure of persecution. Law after law restricted and constricted the ability of Jewish citizens to go about their lives. Jews could not practice their profession, own a business, use public transportation, attend schools, use parks or places of recreation, or attend religious services, and they could shop only at a few specified hours at the end of the day. Each had to wear a large, yellow cloth star. The Dutch population became increasingly hostile to the German occupiers. In February 1941 a general strike started in Amsterdam and was spread by the working people of the cities and the countryside. Among other strike causes there was widespread indignation about the brutality toward Jewish citizens. In July 1942 the Germans began the deportations of Jewish citizens to Poland and other points east.

The period of spring 1943 to September 1944 saw increasing resistance in the form of another countrywide strike. The Germans put this near insurrection down with sufficient lethal force to stop open resistance. The underground resistance that had been organized, slowly, by leaders in the churches, trade unions, socialists, and communists accelerated. Resisting the forced labor callups, harboring and returning shotdown Allied airmen, and stealing or forging food ration stamps and identity cards were some of the underground activities. Dutch teenagers, political enemies of the Reich, and Jewish children and adults were hidden (*ondergeduiken*)[1] to avoid the frequent raids and dragnets. Once hidden, food ration stamps had to be supplied by the underground. The resistance used sabotage and assassinations. An extremely active underground press emerged during the war years.

The final period of the occupation from September 1944 to May 1945 (the liberation) was desperate. In the northwestern provinces there was famine during the 1944–45 winter because the Germans stopped transporting foodstuffs into these areas; this, as revenge against the resistance.

The Germans had initially attempted to persuade and pacify the Dutch people, but ended with increasingly brutal behaviors. In the last years, death or the concentration camp was the fate of anyone who fell into their hands. Early on an order was put into effect to execute ten civilians for any one German soldier or official who was attacked. Although the German occupiers were not as vicious as the brutal German behavior displayed in Eastern Europe, the occupation was a time of great suffering and for some extreme hardship.

In contrast, the Germans made war on the entire population of Eastern Europe. They were infinitely more savage there than in the west. They made total war on the Jewish population. Young couples with babies, families with toddlers and school-age children, grandparents, teenagers, sick folks, the handicapped—no one was left in peace. Everyone from the newest baby to the oldest soul was hunted down in every corner of the lands controlled by the Nazis. They also made total war on the Gypsies but they, having always lived on the fringes and being of nomadic habit, were able to escape in proportionately larger numbers.

Out of approximately 140,000 Jewish people who lived in Holland, 105,000 never returned after the war. Fewer than one out of twenty (5 percent) came back from the camps. The people in hiding had a better chance to survive.

---

[1]Literally, "to dive under."

My father's family originally came from Poland. Some generations ago one ancestor was a physician in Breslau. He laid the foundation of a public health system by ensuring a clean water supply and a safe sewage disposal system for the city. He was the first Jewish physician allowed to practice openly in the city. My father's parents were mismatched. My paternal grandfather was unable to make much of a living and periodically disappeared. My father and his sister grew up in severe poverty in Berlin.

My paternal grandparents' marriage had been arranged and I believe my grandmother never got over her disappointment and bitterness. She was intelligent and wrote poetry and plays. However, her only outlet was through activities in the synagogue, such as writing the Purim plays. My paternal grandfather died of an unknown illness during World War I.

I do not know how my father managed to get his rabbinic training. I do know that at some time in his youth he worked in a furniture factory. He actually had one year's study at the Hebrew Union College in Cincinnati, Ohio. I suspect that education was the "way out" and that my grandmother was ambitious for both her son and her daughter. My aunt trained to be a pharmacist in Berlin and with that profession was able to emigrate to the United States in the mid-1930s. My father was a true intellectual. He loved the classics, history, and the play of ideas. He was a Zionist as well as a religious leader.

Although my parents' marriage was not arranged it, too, was somewhat mismatched. My mother was born in 1912 to a family of achieving business and professional people. Although there were no artists in the family, music, art, poetry, and literature were much valued. My mother told of being taken as a thirteen-year-old to a glamorous evening at the opera by her own mother. She developed a lifelong passion for classical music. Various relatives could and did quote lines of poetry at auspicious moments. Others were and are passionate appreciators of art, and a few are now collectors. One early ancestor made his living as a horse trader; one great-grandfather was a banker in Berlin. One line of my mother's relatives can be traced to a Swiss village near the Swiss-German border. The generation of my maternal great-grandparents was comfortably established and well educated. Some were observant Jews; others lived a secular life. Some of these relatives fled to Portugal and the United States. Unlike my father's family, this side of my family did not become Zionists. Some family names were Wertheim, Guckenheimer, and Glaserfeld.

My mother was an only child. She was born with a congenital illness that causes periodic fever and abdominal pain, and has many periods of remission and recurrence. It appears most frequently among Sephardic Jews and other peoples around the Mediterranean basin. In the 1960s it was given the name Mediterranean Familial Fever, and a medicine that ensured permanent remission was found.

After my parents married, they moved to Amsterdam. There my father became the rabbi of the large Liberal Jewish Synagogue. He had been recommended for this position by Leo Baeck, a beloved and heroic rabbi and teacher with whom my father had studied. I was born in 1935, and my brother three years later. Both of my grandmothers, now widows, were still in Germany. My mother's father fought in World War I as a German patriot and died of his wounds when my mother was five years old. My parents managed to get my grandmothers out of Germany, and both arrived in Amsterdam with the hope of living out the war with their family. Most of what they still owned was of course confiscated by the German government. This was the political background when the memoir begins.

For a thousand years Jewish people were invited or allowed to settle in various European localities. Then at a politically opportune moment they were driven out. Whether wealthy or impoverished this pattern continued over many years in many places of Europe. The local powers enriched themselves with what the Jews had to leave behind and the Jewish communities were always geared up to help their fleeing people. The Nazis knew very well how in the past the self-governing Jewish communities had dealt with the authorities—princes, bishops, landowners, military commanders. The Jewish communities learned to do whatever might work at a given moment in a particular place. They kept the people safe if possible. When they were driven out they tried to safeguard the wherewithal to make a living in a new place. Sometimes there were massacres anyway. But sometimes there were periods of calm, too, when people just lived their lives.

The Germans knew very well of the extremely close family bonds that were the norm in Jewish culture. When the deportations began the Germans distributed much deceitful propaganda. For example, they assured people that families would be able to stay together. The Germans also dealt with the Jewish council in Amsterdam. A small leadership group was formed to weigh what was more dangerous to the people: some cooperation in order to save the majority or risk massive shootings with no survival at all? For the law-abiding middle-class leadership it must have been a terrible choice.

In Amsterdam's working-class areas, the younger Jewish men fought the Germans in the streets and were killed. The Nazi assault in the media, the public hate rallies, and the endless haranguing of the Jews had worn down the people, especially the German Jewish refugees. In the end, the resistance took the form of slowing the transports, of trying to find hiding places, and taking babies and young children away to gentile families who would take them in. I do not know if my father had any public role during this time. I do know that he believed he ought to stay in Amsterdam as rabbi to his congregation—that he could not desert the people. We were taken later than some, earlier than others.

As a Zionist my father had successfully obtained "papers" from the British government that might at some future time enable us to settle in then Palestine. These papers were worth more than nothing and less than a visa. No one could have foreseen it but the papers gave us a small chance. Without them we would all have been sent to Auschwitz, where my grandmothers were sent.

When I think of my young parents of those days I feel immeasurable sorrow. Europe has never been a stranger to massacre, atrocity, or vicious wars. But those days of my parents' young adulthood were a time of desolation beyond any reckoning. I have always thought that to have believed in the existence of the concentration camp world beforehand, people would have had to have been psychotic themselves. It is only hindsight (so wonderfully wise!) that enables us to see the marker events, to hear the warnings, to question why the British and American governments did not react to the firsthand knowledge they received by 1941–42.

For a thousand years the church and the secular centers of power jockeyed for supremacy. In this battle the Jewish communities were sometimes used as pawns. It is heartbreaking to realize that each Nazi edict against the Jews had some precedent in church law and action in the long years before the modern era.

In the end there is no rational explanation for extreme evil just as there is no explanation for the loveliness and goodness and courage in some people. We are both a terrible and a wondrous species; disastrous and magical. There is no explanation. One can only choose to do one's part in making this world a better place. In Hebrew *Tikkun Olam* means to heal, to make more perfect the world. And a saying of the fathers is, "You are not required to complete the work, but neither are you free to abstain from it."

I was given so much in the first five years of my life by my parents and my beloved Oma. Through them God blessed my brother and me with wonderful physical and mental health. I started life with a sunny disposition and a warm heart. In my earliest years my parents passed on a tradition of the joy of learning, of seeking beauty in music, in the natural world all around and in words. The rich furbishing of the inner mind, of the soul, is the only thing that no one else can ever take away.

1

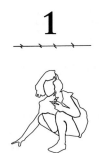

1

MATZA WITH HONEY

The outside stairs are stone and very steep. Then you open the shiny wood door and go up another and then another steep flight. Then our door opens to a square center hallway with a tall grandfather clock that ticks, always. Home—home is where I live with my little brother, Daantje,[1] Mama, Papa, Oma,[2] and Oma Deena.

Daantje and I sleep in a narrow room on the front, streetside of our apartment. He has a crib and I have a big bed that during the day folds up to the size of a wide bookcase, covered with a pretty curtain. On the shelf top sits a collection of dolls but I don't like to play with them very much. Daantje sometimes dreams that big wild animals are coming out of his wall but when I look hard to see them I see only the small pattern wallpaper. I drew small designs on this wall paper because I'm mad at Mama. I know I shouldn't draw on the wallpaper but she has sent me to our room for the afternoon.

Another big room on the front belongs to Oma. Sometimes I go into her room. Once she asked me to thread a needle for her because she can't see the little needle hole so well. When I get sick, Oma says I look green. I look into Oma's mirror, hanging on the wall, but I don't look green at all. Oma tries to teach me not to lisp and asks me to say my name, Sanne. Oma's hair is black and curly. When she gets ready for bed she takes the pins out of her hair and it comes down her back in waves. I like that very much!

---

[1]Dutch diminutive for "Daniel."

[2]"Oma" is the name for grandmother in Dutch and German.

23

The other big room in front is the living room. By the windows stands the table where we all eat together. Even Friday night and Saturday, through the evening meal on Saturday, we sit around this table. When it is not Shabbat or a holiday, the grownups talk about countries: England, France, Germany, Russia, and America. They always talk about the "political situation" but they never talk about Holland where we live. Holland is not big and important so the grownups don't talk about it as they talk about England, France, Germany, Russia, and America.

We live in Amsterdam, Holland, and I speak Dutch. I am Dutch but somehow not like the other kids. I know I'm different but I can't think out how or why I'm different. It's not because I'm Jewish and the other kids aren't because my friends are Jewish and I know they are really Dutch. It has something to do with Mama and Papa coming here from Germany and the two omas who have come here from Germany, too. Sometimes people come to our home and talk with Papa. I know they are going somewhere else but they, too, have come from Germany.

To the left of the central hall are the rooms that have windows to the back, overlooking gardens three stories below. These rooms have doors that lead to the balcony in back where our laundry hangs and where we play. On the living room side there is my papa's study. He is often there and writes or talks with people. Before Rosh Ha Shana he practices blowing the shofar.[3] At first he makes a squeaky, short, quivery sound. Then it sounds deep and full. I can hear it inside my body. Papa has paper clips on his desk. I sneak into his study and take them to make a long chain of paper clips. These will make a perfect throwing piece when we play hopscotch. The chain has a special feeling; I think it will help me win.

On the other corner off the hall is our bathroom and our toilet in a separate little room. Then my Mama and Papa's bedroom. When I was very, very little I stood by the doorway looking at Mama who is sick. Oma stands by me and says I can't go into the room or stand by Mama's bed. Mama is sick and feels far away. I look at her and know I can't go to her. Mama is often sick but Oma takes care of everything. Oma takes care of me a lot of the time.

In the middle, opposite from my and Daantje's room, is the kitchen. It is narrow, too, but Oma cooks and our maid works there. I like to watch; Daantje does, too. Oma stirs and chops up onions, sometimes

---

[3]Rosh HaShana is the Jewish New Year. The shofar is a ram's horn sounded at key ritual moments in the New Year and Day of Atonement service.

parsley. She holds the big knife down on the wooden board and with both hands pushes it in chopping motions that makes the parsley come out very fine. The laundry is boiled in a big, big pot and Oma stirs it.

I like eating in the kitchen with Oma. On Shabbat and the holidays I like eating around the big table. But other times, I don't like it at all. Mama sits on the side and I sit next to her. She wants me to eat everything and gets angry when I can't. At lunch a slice of bread is cut into four little squares. When I have eaten the second square I am very full but that doesn't matter. Sometimes we have meat but the more I chew it the drier it gets. It makes a choking feeling in my throat. There is a vegetable that the grownups eat that is pure bitterness. I hate it when we have that. I get angry at Mama too but she makes me eat everything up. I feel very angry when she makes me eat it later at the next meal.

Some things my Oma cooks are so wonderful! She makes soft rice in a ring and inside the ring is chicken with gravy. It tastes so good and travels so easily from my mouth to my throat down to my stomach. When we have applesauce I take little bites out of the separate sections I draw with my spoon. I make a map of my street and the big street I walk on to get to my school.

On Shabbat, our meal is wonderful, too. Everything is different. I wear a pretty embroidered dress from Palestine.[4] I like to hear Papa say the prayers even though I don't know what the words mean. We sing and the last song we sing is always *Hatikva*.[5] We stand around the table when we sing that. Papa says a blessing especially for me and especially for Daantje. I go to stand by him and he puts his hands on my head and says the prayer. The sweetness flows from the top of my head through my arms and my legs. It is always wonderful. After the evening meal we make *havdalah*.[6] There is a prayer, a sip of wine and sniffing a pretty, silvery box full of spices as it goes from Papa to Mama to Oma to Oma Deena to me to Daantje to Papa. Then Shabbat is over and everything is ordinary again.

There is one thing I love that no one else in my family even likes. It is a Dutch candy—salt licorice. You can get it in little round pellets, in

---

[4]The name of the Holy Land before the establishment of the nation of Israel. The Romans named the land Palestina to erase the Hebrew name of the land: Israel and Judah.

[5]*Hatikva* is the national anthem of Israel. It means "the hope."

[6]*Havdalah* means "separation"—it separates Shabbat from the new week that is beginning.

diamond shapes, and in long strings. When I walk to school I especially like to munch the long strings. Once, on my way to school, some big kids gave me licorice. I plopped a chunk into my mouth waiting for the waves of delicious taste. Instead a sticky bitterness yucked the top and the sides of my tongue. It took me a minute to realize I had a chunk of fresh tar in my mouth.

One morning in May our bedroom window is open. The sun shines and the wind blows. I can look out of our window to the next corner. There our street crosses the Stadionweg. On this wide street are big apartment buildings that have stores on the ground floor. I hear a thudding, thumping noise that goes on and on. Soldiers have come! They march down the Stadionweg endlessly. After a few days there are little red and white striped huts on many of the street crossings. In front of each little hut is a soldier who holds a gun. Now when Oma and I walk we have to go by the soldiers.

We pass by a pool with a fountain. The water fills the pool afresh and the boys sail little boats across the pool. On the far side, we walk through an overhang that is the second story of a school for really big kids. It is dark in the overhang and we have to walk close by a sentry. For some reason I am more scared than I can ever remember being. I hold tightly onto Oma's hand and she says, "It's all right, Sanne." But that doesn't help. My heart pounds and I feel a little sick. Then we are past him and on the next street. That morning in May I am 4½ and the soldiers are the Germans who have invaded all of Holland. They will stay there many years.

When I get bigger I go to the Montessori School. At first Mama or another lady walks us to school. Then I can go by myself. Mama shows me how to cross two streets from corner to corner so that I don't go across the streetcar lines that go around the corner from Stadionweg to Beethoven Street. One day, I look carefully and I can go across the other way. I do, it works, nothing happens, and I am tingling with pride. When I come home I am so excited that I can hardly tell Mama fast enough. I feel surprised that I know Mama won't be angry that I didn't obey her, but I know. Will she be proud of me?

Everything about my school is fine. I like learning to read because the story is about a big farm family and all their animals. There are drawings in color with every story. I would like to live with that family on their farm! I like all the blocks, tools, sandpaper letters, sand box, measuring beads, drawing tools, work tables, the outside garden, and everything else at my school. When we go outside to play, we are on the side of our school. The big kids play in the front. The sidewalk in front has small, square paving stones and you can play a lot of games on them.

My best friend is Ursula. She has braids and lives around the corner from me. She is invited to my birthday. When we play at school recess I run, and running toward me is a boy in my class. We run so fast that I know we are crashing into each other just as I feel myself falling backward. Then I look up and see faces looking and calling, "Sanne, Sanne." But I can't yet say anything at all. For a moment suspended strangely I know I want to talk and cannot. At home Mama puts me to bed. The birthday party has to be another day because I hurt my head and have to rest. The disappointment doesn't matter once I have the party because Mama and Oma make us sweet strawberries and cream.

This is the second time I have bumped my head, falling backward. The first time was skating on the Stadion canal; just learning and gliding into a big man. There were a lot of people skating. I didn't know how to get out of the way or how to stop. Of course, now we can't skate anymore. We can't go on to the streetcar either. We can't go to the stores so that it is hard to get food.[7] That's why strawberries and cream are so special!

I ask Ursula to come up to my home so that she can eat matza with me. It is Pesach and for more than a week we eat only matza.[8] What I like most is to have matza with honey on it and that's what I want to give Ursula. She doesn't have Pesach the same way we do and I feel sorry for her. At the seder[9] only the candles give light and it is mysterious to have all the rest of the room unseen. We sit with pillows and each person's face is in a circle glow of light. I have my own *hagaddah* with pictures that move.[10] A wheel moves and with each turn I can see a different plague. The princess of Egypt stands by the river Nile and Moses in his basket

---

[7]Laws proscribing activities for Jews were enforced shortly after the invasion.

[8]Pesach (Passover) is a Jewish holiday celebrating the Jews freedom from slavery in Egypt. Matza is eaten because, unlike bread, it has no leavening in it; according to tradition, the People of Israel were in such a hurry to leave Egypt, they did not wait for their bread to rise. They put it on their backs and let the sun bake it into hard, flat bread.

[9]The seder is the ceremonial meal and service observed in Jewish homes to commemorate the exodus from Egypt and the acceptance of the Ten Commandments given to Moses.

[10]*Hagaddah* means "telling." At Passover the story of the exodus is read aloud from a book called the Hagaddah. By reading the Hagaddah, Jews relive the journey from slavery in Egypt to freedom in the Promised Land.

moves closer and closer as you pull the tab. Daantje is too little read so I am the person who reads the four questions.[11] We sing songs and it is good! I like to hear Hebrew. Some of what papa says I hear over and over. It sings and sways a sweet feeling in me. I want to learn to read and know just like Papa does. I already know how much I like matza with honey.

Mama uses our big table to lay out knitting in big blue pieces. These pieces will become a dress. Oma has shown me how to knit; knit and purl and like magic it becomes a scarf for my pretend dog. He's on wheels and I hold him or pull him after me. Oma knits, too. The best present she has made for me is a winter hat out of brown, red, and white yarn. It has a point and a tassel at the end but most important it has two long bands on the side to tie the hat on my head. These bands can hang loose and I pretend they are long braids. I toss them over my shoulder. I want long braids but ponytails is the longest my hair gets. Mama says it is too hard to let my thick hair grow longer; mostly it is cut just below my ears and held back with a barrette.

One afternoon, Papa comes home and all of us stand around the table looking at sheets of yellow cloth. The cloth has stars with black borders and black letters in the center. They are made to look a little like Hebrew but they don't at all, really. They say Yood, the Dutch word for Jew. Papa says, "Well, they aren't too awful." No one answers him. These stars are to be sewn on our clothes. Not just my coat will have a star, but every dress and every sweater I wear! Bah! Now Oma and Mama will have to do a lot of sewing.

Oma Deena doesn't sew. Up from our apartment is another staircase that goes to a room under the attic; it faces the street and has dormer windows. You can climb on a chair and look way, way, way down to the street. Oma Deena spends time in her room. She writes fairy tales and poems. She wants to tell me her fairy tales. When I sit on her lap and listen, I get wriggly and want to run away. I don't like her stories and I don't like her, either. Once she gave me a beautiful doll with a porcelain face and long black hair. When I play with this doll I am the mama cutting my child's hair. Oma Deena scolds and scolds me, and then Mama. Mama is a little angry, too, because I cut my doll's hair. Lately the grownups snarl and snap at me most of the time. Even Papa, whom I love more than anyone else, gets angry at the slightest thing.

---

[11]By custom it is the youngest child present who reads the four questions that then are explained to the seder participants as the service unfolds.

28

When we eat at the end of a meal, Papa does magic; how does he peel an apple in one long circle? I look and look. He bets with me that when we eat our cherries he'll have more pits than I. I'm eager to play, eager to win. I never do. I know Papa has a trick but the answer to the trick is on the edges of my mind. I never understand.

Once on the street, immediately after a rain, I look up and see a rainbow. So the story Papa told me about Noah and God's promise is right! The rainbow is here to see and marvel at. Isn't it wondrous that my papa knows to tell me that a rainbow is the reminder of God's promise that never again will there be a flood to make all the people in the world disappear.

But I have found out something important about Mama and Papa. Mama and Papa walk with me to the doctor. They each hold my hand and talk to me quietly. I know something is to happen but I don't know what. I feel more and more alarm. At the doctor's office Mama and Papa sit in a little room while I go to another room. In a high chair I am strapped in so that suddenly I know I can't move at all. I am inside my throat and outside in the room. Everything looks red, the ceiling and the walls, but not the chair or the doctor. I hear screaming and barely realize that Mama and Papa surely must hear me. Why don't they come to get me away? Later, at home in bed, I remember they themselves walked me to the doctor's office. More than anything else I feel amazement and I don't understand how Mama and Papa could sit in that little room while I was tied into the chair. It was me screaming and they heard me, didn't they?

Even so, I like to hear the stories Papa tells me. When I am in bed and can't talk after my adenoids are cut, Papa sits by me and tells me stories from the Bible and stories about the Greeks. I can see the big wooden Trojan horse and all the soldiers tumbling out and Achilles riding faster and faster, brave and strong. He is a hero but he can't prevent getting shot in his heel by a swift flying arrow. Is he still a hero after he limps? I like to watch Papa and listen to him at Shabbat services and when he teaches the big kids. We can't go to our big synagogue anymore so we go to small rooms and Papa goes to other people's apartments to teach. Sometimes he takes me along. I sit in a corner and listen but because I don't understand anything, a mysterious magical feeling comes over me as I watch Papa.

At services he wears a white tallis and so does the cantor.[12] Some of the men and boys wear yarmulkes that are made of dark velvet and

---

[12]A tallis is a Jewish prayer shawl. The cantor is the chief singer of the liturgy in a synagogue.

embroidered with bright glowing red, yellow, orange, blue, and green colors. When Daantje was born one day before my third birthday he got such a yarmulke. At his bris, lots of people came to us and talked and laughed.[13] I found out that he would wear the yarmulke at something called bar mitzvah. This seemed very special and I asked if I could have a pretty yarmulke, too, for bar mitzvah. I found out that girls don't have bar mitzvah[14] and I wouldn't get a yarmulke because girls don't wear yarmulkes. I felt jealous. The colors on the black velvet were so wonderful! I wanted one too!

I don't much want to be a girl. I want to be like Papa much more than I want to be like Mama. Beside it seems boys have more fun playing. I don't like being called a tomboy, either. Still, Oma made me two dresses. Each dress has matching underpants so I can play, jump, and climb just as easily as the boys. Although Mama encourages me to do tumbling and running and enrolled me in gymnastics class, I always feel uncomfortable around her. She comes with the other mothers to watch us the last day of the class. When I do my somersaults down the mat, I feel dissolved in shame at her watching me.

I don't understand why I feel so uncomfortable around Mama. I feel bad inside when I am near her. I often am afraid of her. She gets so angry and often I don't know why she is so angry. When I make her a drawing of a house with pretty flower pots in each window I am happy to give her this present for Mother's Day. Mama looks at the flower pots and says "Sanne, they should be flat on the bottom. You have drawn them with pointed bottoms." I see that this is true but her saying that spoils the happy feeling of giving her a present.

Mama doesn't know this but sometimes I secretly change my high-top shoes and wear my sneakers that I hide by the downstairs steps. I'm not supposed to wear sneakers because my legs are crooked and my feet are flat. I don't know why the grownups fuss so much about it. It doesn't matter at all. In my sneakers I run and jump up and down a ledge that

---

[13]Yarmulke (*kipah* in Hebrew) is the head covering worn by observant Jewish men. A bris (*brit milah* in Hebrew) is a circumcision ceremony performed eight days after a Jewish baby buy s birth.

[14]Bar mitzvah means a thirteen-year-old Jewish male. He is considered an adult, responsible for his moral and religious duties. The word is also used to mean the ceremony that confers this status. A bat mitzvah is the parallel ceremony for thirteen-year-old girls, signaling a girl s commitment to Judaism. Invented by Jews in the United States and widespread among many today, it is not considered traditional.

is built along a building in the next street. I hate my hightop shoes. They are black, lace-up, and ugly. My gym shoes give me extra springiness. I soar and can run faster.

I don't know why things have special power. They do, though! Besides the sneakers, one of the dresses Oma made me has specialness. It's cotton, dark, dark green, and on the green little flowers. Papa's paper clips, my marbles, and my pretend dog have . . . not magic but almost, almost magic!

Those ugly black shoes are not the whole story. Inside each shoe is a liner that is supposed to make my foot arch. Mama took me to a doctor. They put me on a table and put white goop on my feet and legs. It molded to me and from that mold Mama learned what shoe and inner sole I should wear. What I myself want to wear is "klompen," the Dutch wooden shoes! A few of the kids wear them but in the city a lot of kids wear regular shoes. Klompen do make a lot of noise. They really "klomp"!

I look across the street. It's raining and I am not playing with anything. I look across the street at the Levinskys' windows and try to understand what I heard the grownups say, "They have already been taken." The grownups say words that I do not understand but I look across the street through the rain and feel despondent.

Here is a mystery without excitement, wonder, answer—only rainy day boredom, disquiet, edginess. Usually, I make a house under the big table in the living room. Sometimes my friends and I make puppets. Mama once got us a box to use as a puppet theater and we made a play for our puppets. I take my collection of marbles but instead of playing a game with them I line them up and march them around. They have to line up in twos, in fours, and go and stop and turn. I yell at my marble troop and boss them around. I boss them in a loud mean voice exactly as I hate being bossed around myself. But now I am not playing but look across the street puzzled.

Once Ursula and I played at her house. We took off our pants and looked at our tuschies. I spanked her and she spanked me. Just then her mother came into Ursula's room angry, so angry! I heard that it is terrible what we play and really how could I, a rabbi's daughter, behave like this? It sounds endless and then she brings lunch for Ursula and me. We sit at Ursula's small table and I can't eat. I am not, am not, going to cry in front of Ursula or her mother. I want to fall through a hole in the floor. I can't and shortly leave. I never played at Ursula's again. We play outside or by my house.

31

Mama had once sat by my bed and said to me that I mustn't play with my body, "that's for later, when you are a grownup lady." Mama wasn't angry at all but still she told me not to do it. I never stopped playing but after that I knew I was doing something wrong.

How did it happen that I can't go to my school anymore? One day I and many of the children and all our mamas are there to say good-bye to the teacher and some of the children and their mamas. From now on we have to go to a Jewish school. I can still walk to school; it isn't very far from the Montessori School. I know a few of the children but not many. In this school we have to sit quietly and do exactly what the teacher says. The room has big windows but it doesn't seem very light. On one wall are photos of Dutch and German Nazis. Sometimes inspectors come to the class to check whether the photos are hanging on the wall.

In front of the class the teacher sits by her desk. In back of her is a little room where she sometimes sends children after she yells at them and slaps them in the face. Across from me sits a boy who always gets into trouble with her. I don't know why. He has dark curly hair and skin that glows and softly red cheeks. I like him. He makes mistakes in arithmetic and she slaps him. I never make mistakes but wonder how bad it would be to get her angry at me. The inspectors come again. The teacher talks with them and laughs and says it hurts her hand to keep us in line. They laugh again and the sound of their voice gives me a sick, sick feeling. At home, I say that I hate her and this school. They don't say anything and then Mama says, "At least you are learning a lot." Bah! Finally, I, too, get in trouble. I have to go to her desk, I don't know what she says but she slaps me and tells me to go to the little back room. When I go there, I find that it's really very nice being away from the classroom. Not bad at all even if you have to take a slap to get there.

Some children don't come to school anymore; sometimes the teachers don't come anymore. Other teachers come but she stays. I wish she'd disappear. When I walk home from school, boys with NSB armbands stop me. It's not so bad; they call me names and pretend that they won't let me go home. Sometimes a grownup walks by and tells them to buzz off.

One afternoon their leader stops me and yells at me, "Tell me your name, your father's name, your address!" He lives in the neighborhood and I think his parents must be NSB, otherwise would they allow their son to act like this? They order me again, about five of them and all

32

bigger than me. I think if I don't do what they say they'll find out and tell their parents who will make the Germans come to take us away. But if I tell them my name and address they'll know where to find us and the Germans will come to take us away! They are shouting at me and I can't figure out what to do. I cry because it seems no matter what I do it will be terribly wrong. An older, bigger Jewish girl walks by and sees me. Soon she hears what's happening. She shouts at the boys and sounds to me like a grownup person. They move away from us and she says calmly, "It's all right, Sanne, you can go home now." I am in awe of her. Suddenly, it's simple, no problem!

I know about lists, transports, call-ups. Isn't that what the grownups talk about? Some people get called up to go work in Germany. Another walk home from school is interrupted by air raid sirens. I know that you have to get off the street when the sirens sound. Will Germans shoot if you're on the street? I huddle in a doorway where a group of grownups are standing. They pull me in off the street and say I must stay until the warning is over—"No, you can't just go home." A lady brings a cookie from her house. Now what? Mama has told me never but never to take anything to eat from a stranger. But this is different. What should I do? I decide that this time it's okay and eat the cookie with small bites of enjoyment.

At night no light must show. The English are flying air missions. Simchas Torah and Chanukah are celebrated by candle glow only.[15] For Simchas Torah, at services, all the children parade around and around behind the men carrying the Torah scrolls. Daantje and I are little, but we are the rabbi's children so we are right at the beginning of the parade. I am entranced. In the mysterious half dark, we walk, prance, sing, and join the grownups—everyone who can celebrate. At night we light one, two, three, four, five, six, seven, and, at last, on the eighth day, light eight candles on the menorah. The extra little candle is the shammas who is like the worker candle to light the others. On a round table under the tablecloth, presents are hidden. I won't remember the presents but I'll remember the special excitement of the candles lit, the songs we sing, and

[15]Simchas Torah means "joy in the Torah"; on this holiday Jews begin reading the Torah scroll (the first five books of the Bible) from the beginning. Chanukah commemorates the military victory of Judah and the Macabees over the Syrian army. According to legend, when Judah went into the holy temple to light the Eternal Light, there was only enough oil to last for one day. Since the oil miraculously burned for eight days and nights, Chanukah, which means "dedication," is celebrated for eight nights.

holding hands as we go around the table, Mama, Papa, Daantje, the omas, and me.

One morning as I am eating breakfast I ask, "Where is Oma?" Oma is gone. Mama and Papa say the soldiers came in the night to take Oma away. No one says why or where Oma is. Then Mama tells me that they came twice before. But each time Oma hid on the back balcony and slipped into one of the rooms as they were looking for her. This time Oma couldn't hide. She is gone. Oma Deena is gone, too. Oma is gone.

I took money once from Oma's purse lying on a round little sewing table in her room. I used it to buy ice cream in a shop around the corner on the Stadionweg. I stood on that corner looking up to our windows to see if anyone knew what I was doing. And once I was furious with Oma. She called me to come up from the street where we were playing. "I will come but not yet" and then suddenly Oma is there, grabbing me by the ear pulling me home. I don't want any of the kids to see me being pulled home! I'm so angry with her but later not. She helps me wash by the wash stand and before I go to bed I can be in her room. Now, Oma is gone.

We have to go live in a different place! I won't even go to the school that I hate. The new apartment is far away in another section of Amsterdam. Here, too, we climb stairs but not as many. Everything in this apartment is small and dark. Daantje and I have a little room to share. Now I have to cross a plaza and at the opposite end follow the street to the school where I now go. It's not far at all but it's dark and crowded with a lot more children. The only thing that I can understand in this new school is arithmetic. We each have a little slate with a marker and on this slate we write the sums. I find out that when I go up front to show the teacher my work, she slaps me because I make mistakes. I feel surprised because I expect to get the answers right. When I return to my desk, it's at the end of a long row and I'm glad to be sitting far back.

After school I go to visit a new friend. She lives in an apartment with tiny rooms also, but hers overlook a waterway. She is home alone, no mama or papa is there and no oma. I like her but everything here feels strange to me. Even stranger but fascinating is another new friend. She lives right around the corner and has some sisters and blond pigtails. We play on the street and no one bothers us. At my other school, the boys had fights almost everyday with boys from a non-Jewish school who walked by us on the way home. After school all of us collect hard, shiny, black pieces of shrapnel. I don't know what it is but it seems to have magic. It's important to have some pieces that you put in your pockets if you have pockets.

One afternoon I walk home from the new school alone and see that there is a red and white barricade across one of the side streets that runs off the plaza. No one is out on the street, the sun is shining, but it is quiet, very quiet. The stillness is strange.

Mama is by my bed, "Get up, Sanne, you have to get up." Mama asks me to put on layers of underpants, undershirts, and socks. Then I wear layers of dresses and sweaters. I feel stiff. Then my coat goes on and by this time we are in the hallway. At the door are two "green police."[16] Papa stands by the door arguing with them. The green police say something and suddenly the argument stops. Mama helps me put on a rucksack. Then she and Papa take a rucksack and suitcases each and we are outside. But it's the middle of the night! I've never been outside in the night like this. We are not alone; many other people are walking as if pushed along a water rivulet. At the corner I see that other streets are spilling rivulets of streaming people to a main stream of pushing, hurrying people toward where? I hear, "Bye, Sanne, bye Sanne!" I look up and from the top floor, my new friend and her sisters and mama are leaning out the window. One of the soldiers yells at them, and as quickly as I noticed my friends, they pull out of sight and close the window. It feels absolutely strange. I realize the rucksack is heavy because the bands are cutting into my flesh underneath where my arms come out of my shoulders. All around me big people pushing close. Suddenly, I spurt forward to hang onto Papa because the next instant I would have lost Papa and Mama's hands to hold. Now I'm terrified.

We are funneled through gates at a railroad station and end up on the floor of a railroad car. We sit and lie against the suitcases. There are not many others in the railroad car. Where we are going I don't know. It is cold and I can't seem to get warm. Still in the dark, we get off the train and drag off to a barrack.

The dark makes everything mysterious. We walk toward someone in another part of the barrack. The bunks look like wood storage cases in some weird shed. The woman who walks toward us is Oma. Mama and Oma make murmuring noises I don't understand. It is Oma but I don't feel that it is really Oma.

---

[16]The "green police"; that part of the German police apparatus in charge of arrests, mass raids, deportations, action against strikes, and executions. They wore green uniforms.

We have come to one of two camps set up in Holland. This one is a transition camp. From here trains leave for "the east." Papa, Mama, Daanjte, and I will live here for several months. It is 1943 and I have just turned seven and Daan has just turned four.

2

WESTERBORK

After the first few days, I forget that we've ever lived anywhere else. It is so strange here. There are too many people and a thousand thousand kids. The soldiers with guns slung across their backs are called marachausee and they are Dutch. They talk differently from us, though. There are Germans, too. They walk around holding onto the leashes of big German Shepherd dogs. Every day transports come, and often the long lines of people have to stand for hours while the Germans scream at them. If someone tries to escape they turn the dogs loose on them. Or they send them to a place called Vught . . . a terrible place.[1] Escape. . . . We are prisoners now. I understand that.

A small group of children are playing ball. My Papa acts as our teacher. The ball rolls from the field onto the frozen canal. On the far side of the canal is barbed-wire fencing. A soldier holds his gun and watches us. Now, my Papa has to ask permission to get the ball. Almost frozen with fear I watch as Papa gets the ball, climbs back from the canal, and continues to play with us.

Westerbork is big and there are many wooden barracks. Our barrack is filled with bunks, end to end. Between the bunks is a wooden table with benches. This is where we eat and where we live. In the night I have to go to the toilet. It is at the end of the barrack and a long way from our bunks. When I find it, it is disgusting. I can't go there! Mama tied a potty to the rucksack and at night I use that. I'm a big girl, not a baby like Daantje, but

---

[1]Vught was another camp in Holland. It served as an overflow camp for Jews and a permanent concentration camp for others. It had a special women's section.

37

at night it's better to use the potty. One night I awaken crying from a bad dream. Swiftly, Mama lights a candle, I reach over to her and my thick hair catches fire! On the side where my hair is held by a barrette, the bunched hair catches. With a cry Mama slaps the fire out, almost as quickly as it caught. I have peed in the bed; my heart races. In the morning I realize that one of my eyebrows is singed as well as one side of my hair.

Every night lists are read out loud. I wake up and hear families move out into the night. It seems that no one is here alone but maybe that's only because so many people say good-bye or cry or murmur things to those left behind. It is bad to be on the list.

During the day, I begin to go outside and join other kids to run around, explore, and play. I play with a group of boys and girls. We are to watch for an enemy and alternately hunt them or hide from them. I can't figure out who this enemy is! Sometimes I feel the danger but other times it's fun to feel the excitement from some of the older boys and girls. One afternoon I come back to our barrack late. Mama and Papa have eaten and are annoyed, waiting for me. I tell them I have been with my "group" and feel surprised that they don't understand how important that is. After I eat and sit with Mama and Papa, I suddenly realize that I don't understand whether we are playing some game or whether the other group is really an enemy group. I feel confused because I can't think it out. One minute I know absolutely it is real and the next minute I think we are playing.

Daantje and I get measles and we have to be quarantined. That means we have to go to the hospital. This is another long barrack building but it's lighter than the regular barrack. There are bunks on each long wall and a big space in the middle. I can't see Daantje though he's in the same room because he is at the very end and I'm in the middle. Mama and Papa come to see me. They stand outside and wave. My window has grating on it and they are far away. It's hard to see them. I wish they could come often. The hospital barrack is nicer than the dark place where we live. I get better and go back; Daantje stays longer because they are afraid he had tuberculosis. He hasn't got it really but it's good for him to stay longer. I miss one of the nurses who talked to me and joked around. She talks Dutch differently from me and tells me funny expressions. I learn that in Amsterdam slang a thief has "lange yatte." Literally that means "long hands." Yatte is like the Hebrew word *yadim*, which means "hands." Amsterdam slang is full of Hebrew-derived words. Even our affectionate nickname for Amsterdam, "Mokum," is from the Hebrew word *Makom,* which means "place," or "the place."

After some weeks Mama and Papa get sick. They have something that makes them turn yellow. Lots of people are sick with this. But now Daantje and I have to go live in the orphanage.

Unlike the hospital, the orphanage is a very dark place. But there are separate rooms. We have three bunks standing in a U shape and a big chair in the open space. I sleep on the top bunk. Next to me is a pretty girl with curly blond braids. She seems to have been here for a long time because she knows the lady who takes care of us. One afternoon we sit on her bunk and she shows me something special. She has a little picture in a small round frame. This is her mama. Her mama went away on a "transport" but soon she, Rosa, will go too, and then she will see her mama again. Rosa is very sure about this but I feel funny inside when I think about her mama so far away. I'm glad Mama is somewhere in the hospital, here in Westerbork.

We talk and play in and around the bunks. I lean out of my bunk eager to hear and bang my ear against the metal post of the bunk as I fall from the top to the floor—no, not the floor. I land in the big chair, dazed, with my ear throbbing. I could feel the coming crash but bounced into the chair instead. Hard to believe I landed safely in the chair.

We eat in a dining room at tables with long benches on each side. At one end of this room is a stage. Sometimes the director stands there and talks to us but I understand nothing of what he says. I don't know where Daantje is. It is cold now and gets dark early in the afternoon. When we are inside and when we eat there is a light on the stage but only a candle here and there on the long tables. There are prayer books and with each meal some grownups and some children say prayers I don't know. Once, when my book falls, a boy explains to me I have to kiss it and say a prayer as I pick it up. I've never heard of this before. But he says he's Orthodox and that's what you have to do.[2] Some of the kids here are Jewish in a different way from me. It's a mystery!

I don't like the orphanage. The lady who sleeps near us is nice but a lot of the other grownups aren't. One evening before we eat, the director hauls a boy onto the stage. The boy is crying and I think one of the grownups has been hitting him. I don't know what the director is shouting about. I hate seeing and hearing the angry voice and the gulpy crying of the boy.

When Daantje is with Mama he gets temper tantrums. He lies on the ground and screams. Once, at home, he threw something at a mir-

---

[2]Orthodoxy is the most observant branch of Judaism.

ror in the living room. I got scared that time! Mostly I feel sorry for Daantje because Mama seems to get so angry with him. But sometimes I feel angry inside like he gets angry outside and then I just want him to stop. Shut up! Shut up! When Daantje is with other people he doesn't scream.

After a long time the weather gets warmer. Mama and Papa get better and Daantje and I can leave the orphanage and go back to Mama and Papa. I feel bigger. I roam around and play outside the barracks. We explore other barracks. There are soldiers patroling around and one rides horseback. She has a riding crop and wears riding breeches and gloves and she seems always to be around. She yells bad things. Once, while I am squatting in the grass to pee, she rides by and sees me. She yells that I'm a dirty little J—! She yells and yells and I can't move until I'm finished. First, I feel terrible shame but then I remember why I'm peeing outside instead of using a toilet. There is a wooden barrack that has a latrine. There are lots of places but too many people use these spaces. When I try to go there it's too filthy to touch. I try to climb up and stand over the hole. Then, when I squat maybe I won't have to touch any of the wood. When I try that my legs aren't strong enough to hold me for the time I need. So then I decide to do it outside. That's why I'm peeing in the grass! I hate that woman on the horse. She's Dutch but she's a Nazi and I hate her!

In the barrack, around us, all around us are other families. Some families are quiet but some have constant "scenes." Mostly, that means the father or the mother is raging at a kid and it ends up in blows. Then the "scene" continues because the kid cries and the mother and father want quiet and are furious because the kid is crying. I notice that the "scenes" are more often with boys than with girls. Maybe it's better to be a girl. Boys sure get hit more.

Mama and Papa ask me one day if I understand the German they are speaking to each other. I do understand but I don't want to. In the most convincing way I know how, I say I don't understand and I don't remember German from when I was very little. When they ask me to say something in German, I make sure that I pronounce it as if it is Dutch. I try hard not to know that language of our enemy. I want to know only Dutch. I want to be only Dutch.

Every day new people come to the camp and many nights the lists are read. Papa knows how to keep us off the list, doesn't he? I know he does. I don't even think about it. But one night we, too, are read from a list and again we carry the rucksacks and Mama and Papa also carry a suitcase. From some other kids I've learned a song—I know only part of it and it sounds in my head:

> Wij gaan naar Polen!
> met kapotte zolen . . .[3]

There are long verses but I don't know them. I don't even think about where we are going—only that I must stick by Mama and Papa and Daantje so that I don't have that terror feeling of losing them.

---

[3] We go to Poland/our shoes are worn and broke . . .

3

FIRST DAYS

The train is a compartment. The windows are blackened so that you cannot see in or out. We ride through the night. Miserable, I sleep on and off. The train stops on the railbed that is built higher than the surrounding country. The doors open. There are German soldiers everywhere, holding onto barking German Shepherds. The Germans scream, "Schnell, mach schnell, raus schwein hunde!"[1] Hurriedly, everyone scrambles out of the train over the gravel and stones of the railbed. I understand their words. I am liquidy inside with terror.

It is dawn. There are really not that many people stumbling off the train. Someone is pushing a woman in a wheelchair. And another family has an idiot person they hold onto. We have to line up and walk to wherever we are going. It's heavy to carry the rucksacks and suitcases. The Germans scream at us. When people fall they beat them with a club. The dogs are everywhere. Do they bite and eat up the people who fall? "Oh, walk, don't stumble, don't fall, stay with Mama, stay with Papa, walk, don't stumble, don't fall, don't fall. . . ." There are so many Germans! It is far.

"Walk, don't stumble. Walk to that little stone, then that one, then the next one, don't fall, don't stop, don't be tired, walk. . . ." I don't see anything besides the road, the dogs, the Germans, and the back of the people in front of me. I don't hear anything but the screaming, cursing Germans, the whining, growling dogs, and the shuffling feet of the people around me.

---

[1]"Hurry, hurry up! Get out, pig dogs!"

42

Sometime that day we turn into a huge empty space. It is enclosed with barbed wire, and behind that another barbed-wire fence. The first fence has little white porcelain-looking knobs spaced on it. Electricity goes through these. In between the two fences are rolls and rolls of barbed wire.

We have to stand in this open space for a long time. I look up and in the far distance behind the barbed wire, there, where the forest begins, stands a tall tower of wood. It's a watchtower, and in each is a German with a gun. There are many watchtowers. The open space has gravel on it, fine gravel, but there isn't a single green thing growing. Only very far away on one side you can see the dark green forest. So we stand, a small group of people in a very big empty space.

The Germans are all around us. One of them begins to yell something. He goes on and on in his scream voice. Papa turns to Mama and says, "It doesn't look like this will be much better than Westerbork!" I can't believe my ears. How can Papa even think that! Say that! Isn't it obvious that this place is already more terrible than anything? Grownups are crazy! But Papa, how can he say that?

Finally, we go to a barrack. No one is here but our small group from Holland. Most of the barrack is filled with three-tier bunks. One part has tables with benches and a small black potbelly stove. On one wall are some wooden storage lockers just big enough for a person to hide in. The men have to go to another barrack in another section of the camp. People have brought a little food with them and that is what we eat. Papa isn't here but we go to sleep. The next night the men can come when people eat but they can't stay with us. The Germans come and scream for everyone to leave, "Raus! Raus!"[2] I notice one man hide himself in one of those lockers. The Germans come back into the barrack and fling open all the lockers doors and he runs out. They hit him from behind with their clubs. He holds his arms over his head. I am so glad Papa didn't try to stay.

When I wake up Germans are in the barrack! Almost all the people are dressed and hurrying up. Oh, we must make the bed look tidy and we must hurry outside. I look down the row of bunks. Already the barrack is almost empty. Down a far row a German is yelling at a young woman. Her bed isn't made right. He hits her face over and over and screams. Outside, we have to line up a few rows deep. They are going to count us! The children who are smaller have to stand in the front row so

---

[2] "Get out, get out!"

the Germans can see them. If the number isn't correct something terrible will happen. I am very, very afraid to stand in the front row but that is what I have to do.

Now I see that there is one other group of people here already. I listen to the grownups and learn that these people are from Greece, Jewish people from Greece. What I really notice is their leader. He is a big, big man and he talks to the Germans. When the soldiers are asking questions or yelling orders they turn to him. I think he is very brave.

The Germans never talk. They scream everything at us. Mama mutters that on top of everything else, the Germans are determined to destroy the German language. I know that Mama knows poems and even German songs that sound sweet and give me a lovely melty feeling inside. But I don't understand what Mama means by "destroy the language." I see that she is very upset.

In our barrack is a woman who is Mama's age. I think she is beautiful. She has black hair and she is the one who talks to lots of people. She helps them to choose their bunks and calms them. She organizes how we take the metal barrels of food and ladle soup into the people's bowls. Every family takes a turn dishing out the food. In return that family can scrape out the bottom of the barrel. The water of the boiled turnips is thickened. When we scrape the barrel the thickened leftover film on the barrel makes a whole other bowlful to eat. It is much better to eat than the turnips.

Mama and I have a turn. The barrels are outside. I notice the little white clouds in the sky so high and far away from us. The sun is low and the sky has beautiful colors. It is quiet. No one is screaming. I help Mama scrape. We get a bowlful of thickened soup. Oh, it's good to eat this. I feel a throbbing, glowing, strong sureness coursing through me. Pushing from the inside of my body to my arms and legs. I know I am strong, good, soaring with pleasure feeling. I know—oh, I know I am going to be all right! The feeling is so sudden and so intense that I look around to see what has happened. Nothing has happened. There is Mama and there is me, scraping the food barrel. There is the wonderful sky. So high, so big across the distant space. Far away is the forest. Nothing else.

4

APPEL IS FOREVER

I learn from some bigger kids to find a stick. Then you find a little piece of wood. You hit the little piece hard on one side. If you do it right then you can make the little piece jump high and it falls down at a distance. You can try to flip your piece to the line the other kid draws on the ground and they can try to flip it to your line. I'm outside flipping my little wedge of wood but I don't do it long. It feels dangerous to be out in the empty space. There are just a few other kids outside. Every time a German comes we run away. As we run, Daantje gets mad at me and throws little stones at me. He's my brother, he is not supposed to throw stones at me!

I learn other things listening to the big kids. They say that if you eat standing up instead of sitting down then you'll feel full. Then I overhear one girl say to another, "I'm not asking my Mama for more to eat because I know she can't get more. It'll just make her feel bad." I'm so surprised to hear this. I never would have thought of that myself, but now I decide that I, too, won't ask for more to eat so Mama won't feel bad.

In a rucksack hanging by our bunk I discover a jar with jam. Once I open it I run my finger around the edge and put it into my mouth to taste the wonderful sweet. Again, another taste, just a little swipe. I check again and again to see if the level of the jam jar is going down. And it doesn't! Oh, I shouldn't keep tasting. Mama brought this for all of us. I'll stop . . . just once more this wonderful, wonderful sweetness. Suddenly, I see that the level of the jam is really lower. Oh, how did this happen when I just looked a minute ago! Now I really have to stop. Quick, I close the lid, put the jar back in the rucksack and run outside.

Every morning as we wake up Germans come into the barrack and yell, "Raus, raus!" We have to go stand outside in the big, big empty space. Each barrack has to stand together, children in the front, so that each day they can count us. Each day something is wrong with the counting and in the distance I can hear the Germans screaming at the man who is the spokesman for us. Sometimes the spokesman is the big Greek man. He seems to know what to say to the Germans. Mostly, the counting is wrong so we have to continue standing while the Germans come slowly pacing around again, looking us over. My heart almost stops when they pass by me and Mama and Daantje. This standing outside and being counted is called appel. Every day we go to appel.

After we have been here some days, I notice that the women around us in the barrack are taking sheets and underpants to a wash house standing near our barrack. Mama is sick so I take the sheets and underwear to the washhouse. I watch the women. I put everything into a sink. It fills with cold, cold water. I stand on a bench to reach into the sink and try to wash. I can do that but how do I get the sheet out of the water? When I try it's so heavy that I can't even hold onto it. After I try for a while someone I don't know comes to help me.

Now, all the women and all the men leave the compound everyday after appel. They go to work. The only people who stay are the small children and the mamas. In the evening we have appel again because now the Germans want to count us again after the grownups come back from work. During the day, the Germans come into the barrack. The women try to run away and I learn to run with some other kids into a different direction. The barracks have doors at each end. Some of the women and kids make a confusion so that the Germans have more than one person to chase. The women are frightened, upset. Mama is, too. Something bad will happen but I don't know what. After a while the Germans disappear again.

In the barrack there are so many people and lots of children. But outside when we stand surrounded by German soldiers we are so few people. We are lost in that empty appel space, lost in dangerous smallness, few of us; many of them with their dogs, their guns, their clubs, their scream voices.

I don't know the people around us. I do know a small group of girls as old as me. Really, I know only two of them, Bat Sheva and Lisa. Lisa shows us icky sores on her arms. She says she has them all over her and she's had them since Westerbork. I look at her and am so glad that I don't have these pussy sores all over me. Bat Sheva is pretty. She has curly black hair and snappy black eyes. I admire her. She also has a brother, Moshe, but he is older than she is. I think it would be much nicer to have a brother, older, than a brother who is practically a baby! We don't play but we talk about things. We watch a lady who has a real baby boy talk to her baby. When she takes off his wet clothes, the baby pees in a big arc that reaches way over to the other side of the bunk. We laugh and love to watch this baby.

The best, though, is sitting on the outside steps of the barrack with some older kids. I listen to them talk and that seems wonderful. They talk about what they will do if the war is ever over and we get out of this place. They talk about going to Palestine and about being a teacher or nurse or doctor. I only vaguely understand what they are talking about. But I think they will make everything okay when they are the grownups and the war is over.

One morning the Germans call out names, and the families who are called have to gather together separately from the rest of us. Unbelievably, I learn that they are going to get away from here because the Germans are going to trade them for German POWs! These families have papers from the British that say that one day they can go to Palestine. The "papers" make the trade possible. Papa has "papers" for us. Will we get traded, too? The people stand with their rucksacks, close together across a vast distance from the rest of us. I look and look and what I feel is beyond jealousy. Only a desperate disappointed longing. This is the only time I know of that someone gets "traded."

On appel, I notice that people keep coming. Instead of a few people in that empty space there are people lined up at a distance farther than I can clearly see. When the men and women come back from "work" some awfulness always happens. Right by us the Germans stop and yell at a man. The club crashes on his head. Blood rivulets open slowly. On his forehead, a river is made by his blood coursing this way, then that way. Appel goes on and on. It is hot in the sunshine. Hot and thirsty; appel holds us. I think the Germans are the cat and we are the mouse. Cats play endlessly with the mice they catch, always finding new ways to hurt them. On some days appel is all day. We stand and wait. We wait until evening when the workers come back. Appel is forever.

I notice two Germans particularly. I notice them because they are always there and are especially dangerous. One is tall and wears horn-rimmed glasses. He actually looks like a normal person. But he walks slowly and proudly by us as if he's parading, showing off his power in front of us. Lots of times he has a dog on leash. The other is called "de rooie"[1] because his face is always red. Is his face red because he's always screaming or because he's always drunk? I don't really know what that means but the grownups talk about this one especially and he "is drunk."

We are in another barrack again. This time I share a top-tier bunk with another girl. I don't know her. Mama has Daantje next to her, in the middle bunk in the next tier. My bunk is all the way in the corner by the wall. It is evening and we are lying in the bunks. Suddenly, in a terrible rush, Papa is by us and is climbing up to my bunk! He lies by the wall and I am so, so quiet! The danger feeling is everywhere. I can't breathe; my heart bursts in its beating. The "rooie" is on a rampage. He and other Germans come screaming into the barrack and look for the men they are hunting. My skull's top will explode away from my head if this terror-fear lasts one more second! In my head is a screaming . . . the "rooie" comes right between the bunk tiers where we are; Papa scrambles away. I hear shouts and screams outside. I am terrified what will happen to Papa out there in the night. At the same time the relief from the terrible fear is slowly trickling through me. It takes a long time before my head feels all right again and I can breathe. Mama mutters up to me from her bunk, "Why weren't you quiet!" Oh my God, is it true, did I make a noise? I thought the noise was only in my head—I don't know, I don't know if I did. Is it my fault the "rooie" caught Papa? Is Mama really saying that to me? Oh God, oh God, I can't scream, I can't cry. I can't faint. I only feel agony and confusion. I don't know what really happened. Papa, Papa, I don't know.

In one of the next days, Papa comes back to our compound. He talks with Mama briefly. I overhear something about the forest. In the forest the men are driven to work. "De rooie" beat the men. Something happened to Papa's back. I can understand only a word here, a phrase there. In my imagination I see the men running, covering their heads against the clubs.

More and more people come. There are children everywhere. Sometimes I roam around and notice so many of the people are mysteriously different. They speak languages I haven't heard before. If you watch from a distance you can see that they are different with each other than we from Holland are. In summer, at evening time, their strange sounds and strange ways of being add to the unknowingness feeling that comes over me when I am alone, outside, at dusk. Not only are the Germans ununderstandable but it is as if everyone in the world is unknowable.

---

[1]"The red one."

A new transport comes from North Africa. The people look different. They are browner and the children are dressed in thin summer clothes on their thin, fine-boned bodies. One day I notice that all these children are bossed by their teacher who carries a thin wand. What are they doing? They walk around their teacher in a circle, around and around. They are chanting something but often he switches at one of the children. I am very, very glad I'm not one of them. Later, I don't see them any more.

It is crowded now. Often we have to move from one bunk to another. This time we get one bunk for Mama and another for me and Daantje. Mama is far away from us. Daantje and I are in a middle bunk; together we sleep end to end. I get mad at him and kick him. He kicks back. But I'm bigger and stronger. I hurt him sometimes and feel mean. One evening Mama and Papa come to our bunk. Together, they show me a piece of bread cut up into many little pieces with sweet jam on it. Where has it come from? What are they doing? Mama and Papa tell me that this is for me because today is my birthday. I am eight years old. The bites of bread are absolutely wonderful. But, oh, they are gone so quickly! In my belly is a pulling, drawing achiness. For a moment I was surprised, happy. Now I feel a misery nagging at me as if I'm remembering something important without being able to remember what it is at all.

Days later I'm standing between bunks listening to a woman explain to me that Mama fainted. She is lying in a bunk, fainted. I'm almost sure that "fainted" is not "dead" but really I'm not sure at all. I don't know how to know the difference. Mama lies still, her eyes are closed. My heart beats. The slow, heavy beats knock in my throat. In all my body the pounding beats knock against me. When Mama moves and makes a noise I know that she is not dead.

One afternoon I cross the appel space by myself. No one seems to be around. The commandant, the one with the horn-rimmed glasses and fine, tidy uniform appears. He is walking right by me. I see the shiny high leather boots, the belt and leather straps to hold his gun, the insignia on his cap, his solid strength from having food to eat. I see it all in less than a second. He says, "Have you a kiss for me? I have just such a little one as you at home." In his voice is a wanting something, longing . . . what for? Whatever for? He wants? From me? I can choose *not* to give something? All the hate and contempt I have in me for the Germans I let him see on my face. I hope it shines out from my eyes. I try to walk as straight as I can, away from him, slowly. It takes all my self-control to walk slowly and not bolt away. I expect a club on my back any second. As I walk I flood with a power feeling; it helps me not to run. The power feeling is so strong and so new that I never after forget it. I never again feel it. It's as if a moment's knowledge of another way to exist touches me crossing the appel space.

5

WINTER

It's now cold at appel. Sometimes it snows in heavy, wet flakes. Mama goes back to the barrack. She cries, and in between cries she mutters curses at the Germans. She gets Daantje out to stand appel in the cold, wet snow and I've never before heard Mama say the bad words she says now. Daantje has an ear infection. He gets hot and cries because his ear hurts so. But today the Germans are throwing all the sick people out in the snow. Mama goes to get him before they do.

One very cold day, a new transport of people arrives. They are from France. I think they must be from very far away south where it never gets cold. The women and children wear cotton summer dresses and slippers or sandals. Across the appel space I notice a girl, maybe my age. I like how she looks but she must be so terribly cold! I suddenly think to run across the open space to give her my hat. But, oh, I can't do that. If the Germans see me, they'll find out who my Mama is and who my Papa is and then they'll punish them. I think that. And so I don't run across to give that French girl my hat. I hate being not brave enough to run across the appel space!

Now that it is cold and wet, appel is even longer. Often it is dark night before we can go back to the barrack. One evening I cry softly. Oh, I don't want to cry but everything in me is cold, wet, and drawn together in hunger hurt. Appel is over but it's so far to walk back to the barrack. It's still snowing. My feet squish in my icy, wet shoes. I begin to listen to what Mama is telling me. Mama says my body is just like a little black stove, just like the one that stands in the barrack. Like a little stove my body needs fuel. When we get back she will give me and Daantje some food she still has. And then just like a little round stove that gets hot and glowy as the fire burns, I will feel warm and glowy good.

When we sit on our bunk, Mama gets a container out of the rucksack. She gives each of us a spoonful of the most delicious tasting food I have ever eaten. I don't know what it is. Mama tells me it is oat flakes mixed with cocoa and sugar. We get one other spoonful. Not just my tongue but my whole body is slurping in the wonderful taste. I have never, never before had anything so exquisitely delicious.

Sometimes the men can come to our compound. Their compound is right next to ours. There is a huge double barbed-wire gate. Sometimes the gate is open, sometimes closed. Papa is sitting with Mama, Daantje, and me. It is snowing again. The snow is packed on the ground. I take off my shoes. I walk to the doorway and go outside to walk in the snow in my bare feet. It is very important to me to try this and find out what it feels like. I can do it but there is a burning sensation on my feet. Mama and Papa call to me. They look at me. Why don't they understand how important it is to test out what the snow feels like? I myself am sure that soon I'll be barefoot in the snow. Like the other kids, I have the front of my shoe cut away so that there is room for my toes. But soon my shoes are going to fall apart even if my feet don't grow bigger. That's why I want to find out what the snow will feel like.

By a wooden table, outside between two barracks, I sit with about four other children. A woman I vaguely know is getting us together to teach us. I hardly know what she's talking about and refuse to say anything to her. It seems that once upon a time I knew these numbers but I can't get a clear hold of what I once knew. Besides, I think she's crazy. Who cares about numbers! Stupid grownups! Sure enough, two Germans are coming toward us and I've already run. One of the boys I know tried to go up some stone steps and run into the barrack but a German comes out, swears at him and knocks him down the steps. He goes rolling over and over. I'm glad they hit him so hard. I hate that boy. I feel my own viciousness and I don't care. I run through a wash house and don't see another German until his leg trips me. His arm is raised, he holds a belt, I spring away, and am totally surprised that I slipped out of his grasp.

The grownups try to organize the kids to teach us. At least they've tried two or three times. It's too dangerous. The Germans always come and beat up anyone within reach. A long time ago, we kids sat together, little kids in front and big kids farther back. We were inside a barrack. I thought, "It's a trap." When the Germans came in I ran. Because I was so little and in front I got away outside. Idiot grownups. But once a grownup did a nice thing. She read to a few of us from a Dutch book called *Afke's Tiental*. That book told about a poor boy, one of ten children who grew up a long time ago in Friesland. His family is so poor that often the children are hungry. But his Mama is good and tries to take good care of the children. I loved listening to that story. So, other children have been so hungry? In the book, all the children are all right and good things happen to them in the end.

Are the Kapo worse than the Germans? The Kapo are men who have been prisoners for a long time. They can come and go through the big entrance gates to our camp. Pieces of colored cloth are sewn onto the back of their striped uniform. They are worse but they are not as dangerous as the Germans. They come into our compound every day. Their faces and heads don't look right. They don't look like normal men look. What is it? I recognize who the Kapo are right away but what do I recognize? They beat anyone.

Outside of the barracks is a wooden table. At a distance I walk by there. I see a Kapo lying on top of a woman lying on a table. In the evening in the barrack some women are arguing. They seem very angry with someone. It seems a woman can be with "them" and get some bread.[1] Fantastic! How do you get extra bread? And why are they so angry? If I knew how to do it, I wouldn't hesitate for a minute. But wait! These women they talk about with contempt and bitterness go with the Germans? The Kapo aren't the Germans but they are just as vile. So you shouldn't do anything with them even if you can get bread. Now I lie in my bunk and listen and don't know anymore what I'd do.

At evening time, when we are all in our bunks, the women talk. They talk about what they once cooked and what they once baked. They tell each other detail by detail the ingredients of a recipe. It reminds someone else of what they cooked and the ingredients they used. I hear food names I don't know and can't imagine. I don't know why the women talk endlessly about their recipes. It doesn't help me not to be hungry. My whole body has hunger. The hunger ache is in my stomach, my head, my arms, my legs. I can't make the hunger hurting go away. Before I go to sleep, I think to play with my body. That doesn't help. Nothing, nothing, nothing I think or do can help.

Sometimes, at evening time when we are all in our bunks a woman starts to sing. A song, the melody sweet and sad. The words I don't

---

[1] The ration was one bread slice per day. The bread was made partly with sawdust. The other ration was one bowl of old turnips cooked in water.

understand, but a song. It is wonderful to hear the song. Sometimes a few other women sing. One song is "My Yiddishe Mamme." I almost understand it. My Mama never sings in the evening. But I have been with her during the day when she sings a song. It is called "Roslein auf der Heide."[2] I don't mind that it is a German song. Mama sings it and it sounds lovely to me. Later, in days to come, Mama doesn't ever sing. No one sings at all.

One morning on appel, I look at my coat and see the star is ripped off. The pullover I have on underneath doesn't have a star either. Oh God, what am I going to do? When the Germans come by our section to inspect us, surely they will notice. Oh God, oh God, what will happen to me? For a while I go stand in the back. If I could stand here behind the rows of others they might not notice me. It's against the rules. Children have to stand in the very first row. The inspecting Germans are still far away, I still have time to figure out an answer. I can't, I can't. Finally, nauseous with fear, I stand in the front. I try to sidle against the grownup in back of me so that I can be half hidden. The inspecting Germans include the commandant and a couple of German Shepherd dogs held tightly on a leash. They come closer, closer right in front. Their eyes take forever to look up and down the rows. I hardly breathe . . . oh God . . . in my head I screech with fear . . . nothing, nothing. I don't breathe . . . they move along. I am safely through appel.

New German soldiers are coming. Mama is upset. Then she tells me that instead of the regular army soldiers they are going to bring the SS[3] to do the ordinary soldier things here. And the SS are much, much worse! I don't understand how it can be worse but Mama is upset. The regular *wehrmacht* soldiers have to go fight in Russia.

One morning I sit on our potty next to our bunk. I try to bm and nothing comes out, not even liquid. I feel funny, something is very wrong. I am falling out of myself! A part of me is hanging out. Is this another way to die? Mama notices and looks; she pushes at me and says she got everything into me, into the inside again. My gut was falling out. I feel as though I've stopped dying. I don't understand how you die but there seem to be many different ways to die. I have no feeling in my hips. I pinch myself, hard, to try and make it hurt. Nothing happens. I don't feel

---

[2] "Little Rose upon the Heath."

[3] *Wehrmacht* was the regular army (as opposed to the Gestapo, the SS, and the waffenSS—an army branch of the SS). The SS were elite Nazi troops, shock troops entirely dedicated to death and destruction.

it. I think, "Do you die a little part of you at a time?" I don't know the answer so I'm scared when I notice something funny with my body.

New transports come all the time. Our compound area is made smaller and often we have to move to another barrack, crowded together two or three to a bunk. In the new compounds next to ours I see Russian POW, Jewish men, and Jewish women. The groups change; sometimes a whole group is suddenly gone, their space taken by another prisoner group.

The compounds are separated by rolls of barbed wire and the barbed-wire fences are very high. There is one light that throws out a cone of light. The space around and on the sides is in darkness. Today it snows, wet, thick flakes that veil where I try to see. It is afternoon and already dark. I am standing by this fence to watch new women come into this compound. I am absolutely sure that Ursula will be on this transport. Ursula, my friend from so long ago. Today when I awoke I knew I would find her again. I have already been watching for a while the shadowy, huddling figures. It is too far to shout back and forth. I just know that Ursula will come soon and that's why I am waiting here. Yes, Ursula will be on this transport, I will see her again. I've known it all today.

Women flit by the fence, they walk by slowly. I shout to ask if they know Ursula, have they seen Ursula? No one answers. I wait. It is already pitch black and still snowing. I do not doubt that Ursula will appear. I wait. Suddenly, I look at the many women milling around and I see that I don't know them, any of them. Ursula is not on this transport. Ursula will never come. I won't see her again. Ursula is dead. Now I walk back to the barrack because now I know. Ursula is dead.

The Germans bring a truck, enclosed, into our compound. The word is that if we give our clothes to them, they'll put them in the truck and delouse everything. Some people give a piece of clothing. I don't, I don't believe them. They'll probably make it worse, that's what I think. During this same time we are told to prepare to march to a bathhouse where we can wash. Everyone who can walk is to go. The first time, I go with Mama. This is the first time we have been outside the big entrance gates. I huddle close to the group of marching women and children. Even though I don't know where we are going or how long we have to walk, I'm not as terror-stricken as the last time I walked this road. I know they club anyone who can't keep walking. But I don't see, I don't look. A picture is in my head . . . to fall into the snow and not care at all because where I fall is my outside shell. I look on from somewhere apart. I'll lie in the soft snow and not care anymore, at all.

At the same time, it's thrilling to be outside our compound. When we get to the bathhouse building we are pushed into a big room where we have to give our clothes. The building is stone and is very cold. Over the entrance I notice letters chiseled into the building. I can't read them. They look different and I think how far, far away from Holland we must be. We go through the entry room and come into a high-ceilinged, big room. German soldiers guard us. Why do they have to guard us, naked women and naked children who cannot even walk very well anymore?

High overhead there are showers and water comes out. It is cold. The water stops and starts. I don't know exactly how to wash myself but it is almost good. They push us to another long, narrow room. It is very cold. After waiting and waiting, we get our clothes back. German soldiers are there with us naked women and naked children. They go after this woman and that woman whipping them to the wall while we wait. I'm glad I'm little; they aren't paying attention to the children. Clothed, we march again back to our compound.

The second time I go, I go without Mama. I don't even know how I got among the marching group. I try to push into the center of the women because then I'll be away from the edge when the Germans start clubbing people. This time they chase and push us faster, "Mach schnell, mach schnell!"[4] When we get close to the building it seems there is a sea of harried prisoners, with waves and waves of people rushing after us. Almost I fall, I get myself onto a step of stairs leading to one of the entrances. As I step, my hat gets jerked off my head. As it falls, I decide not to reach down to get it. If I reach, I'll be trampled and crushed. I just got myself safe onto the step. But this is *my* hat, that Oma made for me, brown, red, and white with straps that are my pretend braids! Oh God, Oma, I didn't mean to lose it! I can't help it! Now, now, there is absolutely nothing I own. Nothing that is *mine*—I might just as well be naked, as I will be in the shower house.

At one end of the barrack is an empty space without bunks. Soldiers come in and chase a group of us together to stand here. We are all the children of this barrack but there are only a few of us. Most of the kids seem older than me. There is a man and a woman soldier who guard us, *echte rotzakken.*[5]

Why do these two come? For a while they come every day and yell at us. They play a game—they look and "select" some of us to go outside. Outside is cold and it's snowing, snowing. The game is that they

---

[4] "Move! Hurry up!"

[5] "Real bastards."

scream at you and start hitting but you can't fall down. I know it's dangerous to fall down. Part of my mind is looking at us from the side and I see me falling down into the soft, soft snow. In the cushiony soft snow I lie and nothing matters, nothing can hurt me. I am not there at all. The first time they "select" me I know that I must not fall down and if I do I must get up immediately—oh, but immediately.

The second time they gather us I know that I must hide myself; my eyes must look down. I must not move and my eyes must not move. Then I have a chance to be safe. When I try it, it works. This time they don't "select" me. It feels awful because I want to be brave and this is the opposite of being brave. I think I can look them straight in the face and straight into their eyes; that's how I'm supposed to be . . . but I can't be. I mustn't. I feel shame before myself. I *want* them to know I'm still here. I am not a zombie. But I have to go against myself or they'll "select" me again.

6

FOUR MORE WEEKS

In the clear blue sky, high up, so far out of reach, I see the white trails of airplanes. How is it that they are above us and yet don't know what is happening in this place? If they knew, they could come down and do something. Every time I see the white trail in the sky I feel the impossibleness of being down here and someone from the other world actually flying over us. Sometimes, airplanes fall from the sky, the pilots parachute out; once I saw one pilot parachute off in the trees by one of the guard towers. I think they shot him. One night we all had to rush out of the barrack because a plane crashed into one end and everything burned. We spend the rest of the night outside.

That night I wander around and notice one of the French girls. We try to talk to each other without success. She wears little hoop earrings and I am entranced. Soon I lose sight of her. Her earrings make her pretty. I look at myself and see my knees for the first time. They don't look like knees. I can move the bony piece around. When I stand, waiting, I put my hands into the hollow of my shoulders. There are deep hollows there and they make a good holding-on place for my hands. But still, compared to the little French girl, I feel ugly.

I know from the grownups that the airplanes come to bomb Germany. The morning after bad bombing raids or other bad war news for the Germans, the guards are more terrible than ever. There are constant rumors. The only one I understand is that in a city in Russia, the Germans have to withdraw. It is a terrible defeat for them and I can hear in the voices of the grownups that they are afraid of what the Germans will do here to us as a consequence.

The Germans are making us, the kids left in the barracks, go outside to work at sweeping the gravel. It should look ordered, swept neatly. There is so much gravel and the pieces are so small that it is impossible to do. They leave our grownups in charge, who will be in trouble if the "work" isn't done. But I am not doing this! Every day I drift off to the edges of where the group is "working" and then move away. There are other kids roaming around. I hear another rumor, this time from the kids. I don't understand this one either but it gives me a crazy feeling as if whatever holds all of my mind together is loosening, cracking. Someone is telling me that there is another camp where the Germans make people fat but then they kill them and make butter from the fat. I do not say to myself, "That's crazy, it can't be so" and I do not know what "butter" is really made of. I only get that strange feeling in my head along with a panicky thought; "Oh my God, now I better not wish for food because that will be the Germans putting that wish into my mind. They want to make me fat and kill me to make butter."

One day we are all commanded to stand outside looking toward the road that passes the main entrance gates to our compound. I don't clearly see what is out there. Pits full of turnips? The pit is next to a small barrack where the food is cooked. Are these other pits? I don't clearly see. We all have to watch, down to the smallest child. Something more terrible than anything I have seen yet is happening. I can feel it all around me. Are they taking apart a body? Are they hanging bodies? I don't clearly see. Only I know that the horror feeling is worse than ever. But I don't clearly see.

The population of the compounds on either side of ours changes all the time as transports come and go. In the compound that used to be our men's compound long, long ago there are now Russian prisoners of war. I can see one of them playing an accordion. He doesn't play it often or long. I hear it only once or twice but oh, how wonderful it sounds! The Russians seem different somehow than the other transports that have been in this compound. They seem more solid but what do I mean? I don't know, they are starving, too. So how are they different? I don't know. A while back I saw a prisoner come too close to the barbed wire and the guard shot him. I thought it was extra cruel to shoot him but not kill him. Because now he will only die slowly.

I find out that there is a barrack that is like a hospital where someone cooks food that is not turnips. I walk by there and someone I don't even see throws an onion out. I grab it and walk away, eating the onion layer by layer. It burns and makes my eyes cry but I would eat a thousand onions if I could. I walk slowly. The onion burns. The onion is chewed, juicy in my mouth. The onion is something in my stomach. It comes to me, as I walk, tasting, that I can last four more weeks. Only four more weeks! Surprised at myself, I think that I'm not exactly sure how long that is. Where does it come from, four more weeks? Is it something I overheard grownups say? But the thought is so clear to me, four more weeks. But oh, oh God, I don't want to die yet. I don't want to die before I'm big enough to have a baby. If I get big enough to have a baby, I'll be a grownup. I have to live myself, until at least I can have my own baby! How can eating an onion make me think like this? But it's all so sure in me. I can't last much longer—four weeks, four weeks—and I don't want to die before I am old enough to have my own baby. I don't think anything else at all. I just say to myself, four more weeks. . . . It's like walking to the next stone and then the next and then the one after that. That's how you keep going. So if I say four more weeks maybe that's what I'll think to myself—the next period four more weeks, then it's always in front of me and I won't have to die yet.

When I go by the hospital barrack again I find a few carrots on the ground. I take them to bring to Papa. I myself will eat only the little ones. As I walk away, two prisoners across the barbed wire in the Russians' compound beckon to me and shout, "Give us a carrot, give us a carrot!" They cry and cry to me. God, no, they are for Papa. I can't give them a carrot but they cry to me, on and on. It is unbearable! Finally I think, "Yes, I'll give them one but only the smallest, the rest is for Papa." I throw the small carrot as hard as I can and it lands just the wrong side of the barbed wire. The two men push each other to get to reach the carrot. Immediately a few others are there, stronger, pushing out of the way the ones who called to me. Their fighting is horrible to watch. I wish I hadn't even thrown the carrot. I go away from there.

Sometimes we can go through to the men's compound. I always want to go see Papa. As I walk through the open gates with another girl, a small plane comes swooping down toward us. The pilot flies so low to the ground that I can see him, laughing at us. I hold my friend's hand and pull us both down flat on the ground as I see him diving toward us. He aims his plane right through the gates. I'm convinced the plane would have killed us if I hadn't pulled us down. The laughing pilot is the worst. They laugh to show us how they enjoy hurting us. That is what makes me feel crazy.

Again we are at appel, a very small group now. This time the Germans bring along a woman, also in uniform. Slowly, they pace in front of us. I see and hear the woman bite into a big apple. I want to throw myself at her to fight for the apple and to murder her if I can't get the apple. Immediately I think, if I move they will club us down, they will know who my Mama is and club her down. In the silence, I think everyone, all the men and women standing here must have the impulse to get that apple and no one can move. In a way I do not understand, the appearance and viciousness of this woman seem more awful than the cruelty of the men. It is as if I expect it of the men soldiers, as if it's the natural order but she violates some expectation I don't even know I have. The juice of the apple dribbles on the side of her mouth, each bite crunches and is chewed in slow motion. Oh, God, I want to kill her!

The trees and the sky. Both the trees and the sky are so far away. Only my eyes can find them. The trees are fir trees; they look dark green and stand straight up. I look to the trees and wish I could be far away in the green trees. My eyes can escape. I look up to the sky, the blue great space and the little clouds. I get a feeling of going up and farther up into the blue far away from here. I don't think the thought that the trees and the sky are beautiful. And I don't think that the trees and the sky are not human beings so they are good and have not been shown up as the miserable, evil things human beings are. No, I don't think that at all but I often look to the trees and to the sky. The wide, wonderful sky and the black-green trees.

Today we are in the men's barrack. Mama, Daantje, and I are sitting by one table along with a few other men. Slowly, I realize that Papa and some others are making a memory of a seder. It is Passover then? We hold our food tins and it is the usual turnips. It is gray outside and dark in the barrack. Papa says something; others say a word here and there. It is confusing. I know seder was different but I can't remember clearly how it was "before." A man walks by our seated small group and looks scornfully over to my Papa and to us others. He makes fun of celebrating Pesach. I look at him and I look at Papa. In this moment I understand that a person can choose to make a special holiday. It's not magic, it's not inevitable. You can be like Papa or you can be like the scoffing, angry man. It is as if I can feel both ways are the right way to be. Both make sense, both could be how I would choose to be. Both ways? Even the veiled memory of Pesach, the snatches of prayers, songs, and the sitting together, ceremoniously, are all good. But there is hardly any light, it is cold, there is no food, there is no matza. There is only a little time together before we have to get back to our compound. It doesn't feel safe to be here at all. But Papa once more makes the blessing on my head and

61

on the head of Daantje. And for as long as the prayer lasts and I hear his voice, it has the special feeling. After this time, nothing more is possible. No recognition of holiday or Shabbat ever happens again.

SPRING

In late winter, a day of sunshine causes wet everywhere. I stand outside the barrack in the thin sun warmth. Everywhere I look and step is mud or puddles. To the side of this barrack is another wired-off compound. There standing by the wire is a child. I see that it is a Gypsy child. My curiosity goes only so far as to observe her. I do not walk closer to see because I've just noticed that I am not walking anywhere much anymore. I stand in the thin sun warmth and that is enough. Inside the barrack it is dark. The floor is a sea of mud, vomit, diarrhea. I try to climb from one bottom bunk to another until I reach my bunk on the upper tier of the three tiers. It takes too much strength but I try anyway so that my shoes stay free of the wet filth. When I go in I pass a woman stuck between two bunks. There is no space, just enough for a Kapo to be over her. He keeps on beating her over the back. There is no room for her to get away. They are about two meters from me as I hang onto a bunk on my climb back. I watch a minute and move on my way.

Next to me Mama has a bunk in the middle tier where she lies with Daantje. They don't get up. Every day I stand by the food barrels and bring the tin of turnips in water to Mama. Once, as my turn comes, a woman behind me cries to the ladler, "Stir it up for the child, stir it up!" I see that the thickening is on the bottom and by stirring I get some of the thickened water. After that I notice myself and say, "Stir it, stir it."

So many grownups lie in their bunks. They do not move anymore. Mama lies still on her bunk with Daantje next to her. Day after day, she no longer moves. One afternoon I come into the barrack and as Mama sees me she says, "Sanne, get some water." I don't want to get water and turn away. Mama calls to me and pleads with me to get her some water. I cannot bear the look on her face of desperate begging. All at the same moment, I know I must get her water because I can't stand to see her suffering and I feel deep hatred for her weakness, her desperation. I don't want to see it, I don't want to know it.

Again we have to move out of this barrack into another. With each move, the Germans wire another compound closed and squeeze us into a smaller space. Mama doesn't move until the last minute. I leave the barrack after her at the very moment that the men prisoners come into this barrack. Oh, God, some of them are already climbing through the window openings to scramble for the better bunks. I am so terribly afraid of them that I get the strength to move out and wait outside with our one suitcase. I know Papa came to help and Mama with Daantje has gone ahead to him while I wait for them. But everyone is gone. I can see ahead that the Germans are getting ready to close the new gates. Step by step I drag the suitcase to the gate crying from terror. If the gate closes I'll be left behind with this new transport of men prisoners. My terror gives me the strength to keep moving. As I go through the new gates the Germans are closing them and I see Papa and Mama walking toward me. I do not say anything. I do not let myself know or say that they left me behind. That I would have been lost there forever if I hadn't moved myself through the new gates. I do not let myself know how terrible it is to hear yourself crying from utter terror. It is dangerous to know this about yourself.

In the next barrack I get up on a top bunk. Mama gets one next to me. A woman comes and tries to pull me off claiming the bunk as hers. I kick and hit and curse her, determined to hold on. While I keep the bunk, my mind watches in amazement that I'm fighting like this with a grownup. As I'm lying in my bunk, I overhear Mama and another woman comment on the sound of a bird they hear. Is it a cuckoo bird? I don't know; I don't know any birds. They say, "Maybe this is an omen for good luck, this bird means good luck." Myself, I think that's stupid. There is no sign, any sign, of good luck. Good luck? I don't know what that means. Grownups are impossible.

Again we move. This barrack is divided into smaller spaces. Instead of hundreds of people in one big space, we are now in a partition with a small number of people. Of the women in this space almost every one has dysentery. I learn that some people have typhoid fever. I go to get our rations and bring them back to Mama and Daantje. Today there is no thickening in the water so it is only chunks of turnips and water. I almost cry when I eat a piece of turnip. It hurts my mouth; it is like chewing barbed wire. It hurts my gums, it hurts my tongue. Mama begs me to eat a little but I cannot. I just eat the water. Now Mama does something wonderful. She says that she will tell me about when she was a little girl growing up with her three cousins. Mama was an only child but her girl cousin, Reni, and her boy cousins, Hans and Werner, were just like brothers and sister to her. They are all grownup people and they live in America. I listen to Mama and Reni, Hans, and Werner, and Tante Lily, their mother, all become permanent visitors in my mind. The feelings of love and importance Mama has in her voice as she talks about them also come to visit in my mind. I hear Reni is very beautiful, Hans is very smart and sweet and teasy sometimes, and Werner acts like the spoiled baby brother. For a little while Mama's stories make the hurt go away and make me calmer.

The next barrack we are in is a big one again, very big. Mama manages to get a top bunk and I am in the one right below her. I share it with an old lady. I hate that. Now we have a space and a half for us three instead of two spaces. In the morning I have to take each piece of clothing and find the lice. Between my two thumbnails I kill each louse I find. It crunches and leaves a rose stain on my nails. That is from my own blood. I don't want to kill the lice, I hate doing it but they will eat me up if I don't do it every day.

I look at the young woman in the next bunk. She has a big open sore in one of her armpits. A man comes to visit her. I wish Papa would visit us. But in the end these visits don't help. A few days after I first noticed her, she's dead. Did the lice eat that hole in her armpit? One day the old lady is not there anymore. Now I have the bunk to myself. But it is not any easier for me to sleep. Now it is hard to go to sleep because everything hurts. No matter how I lie on the bunk, it hurts my bones. I look at the crook of my arm. There is some flesh there, I think, "I can bite that and chew and eat that. It would still be part of me." It sounds right but as I think it I know I can't do that. It wouldn't work. I feel disappointed with my own thought.

Packages have come from the Red Cross. But there doesn't seem to be much to eat in the packages. Nevertheless, the Germans announce that for some days we do not need rations since we have the Red Cross packages instead. There are sugar cubes in the packages and candles. When Mama lights a candle at night the wax drips softly down the side. I pry if off when it is still soft and eat it.

Mama parcels out the one loaf of bread from the package carefully so that we have something every day. But I wish she would just let us eat everything up at once. What a wonderful feeling that would be. In the next bunk is a family with a couple of daughters. The father came to visit when the Red Cross packages first came and they ate everything up, together. It seemed to me they were feeling happy together. I felt very jealous.

Outside I notice some people make a fire with slats from the few wooden bunks; most of the bunks are made of iron. They heat water and something from the Red Cross packages must go in the water. I don't know what it is. I walk by and ahead of me I see a Kapo kick over the water pots, one after another. I know how horrible they are but this special meanness seems different, like a cruelty of a different order. I feel that fleetingly but I don't think about it.

It seems to me that I've been carrying a tin with rations in it for so long that I can't remember a time before this. I carry the tin to Papa's barrack. Papa also doesn't move anymore. Now, there is no fence to separate the men's compound from the women's compound. There are fewer German soldiers inside the compound. It's wet and cold but sometimes the sun shines. There is no more snow.

When I walk to Papa's barrack, I talk to God. Each day I'm sure that this time I'll find Papa dead. To God I say, "Please, don't let him be dead, please don't let him be dead, I'll do anything, anything, please don't let him be dead." It is a long walk. As I get closer, my heart almost stops, my breath almost stops. I am stilled through and through, braced for what I will find and hoping—oh, dear God—hoping. . . .

I go into the barrack and near the door Papa is lying in his bunk, so still . . . his eyes are closed. I am paralyzed. Then, then he opens his eyes, sees me, and smiles. The smile that awashes me with relief that he is not yet dead. The smile that recognizes me and in that moment awashes me with joy—my Papa's smile for me.

He eats from the bowl. A few other men are also lying in their bunks. They say a few words to Papa. I hear someone call him rabbi. Papa and I hardly talk at all. Once he asks me if I can take the can they use as a latrine out to empty and I say yes.

I carry it by the metal wire handle. It is full to the top with brown liquid. I have to try not to let it slosh over on me. I carry it to the latrine house step by step because it is so heavy. I don't realize that I could empty it on the ground. I don't know that I'm too little to do things differently then "how I'm supposed to." It is very hard to do and the metal cuts into my hand and hurts. The next time I bring a ration to Papa, it starts all over again, "Please God, don't let him be dead . . . please dear God, I'll do anything, please don't let him be dead. . . ."

I can't sleep in the evening and I can't sleep in the dawn. I wake up in the early morning, just as the dawn comes. Since I lie in the middle bunk my eyes are level with the window. I look out and see that across the way men are throwing naked bodies out of the barrack. Then I see a truck come and men throw the bodies on the truck. The pile is high every which way, arms and legs and heads. My first horror thought is what if one of them is still alive? In the early light the skin looks a yellow-gray white, a terrible white as if it reflects the early gray light of dawn. Oh, I know I shouldn't look but I can't not look. It's bad to look, I know it, I know it, but now I wake up morning after morning. I cannot sleep. I do look. I do see.

Just today, I notice something very strange. There are empty bunks in this barrack. It is not crowded with women and children, two or three to one bunk. No, there is emptiness. We are again a small group of people.

I am waiting in line. We have to get a shot.[1] A German soldier and some other person sit by a small table. Each person has to give their arm and is given a shot. I don't want to. It will hurt. I don't want to but there is nowhere to go and I can't even run anymore. After this, we learn that we all have to come to the big main gates. We have to leave the barrack and be there at dawn. Everyone who can walk has to come to the main gates. Where will the Germans take us? What will happen to the people who cannot move anymore? No one knows.

In the evening Mama, Papa, and I walk to the grounds by the main gate. We still have one suitcase. Papa walks and carries it. He hasn't moved for so many weeks I don't even remember how long. Slowly I walk behind them. I think, "Don't carry the suitcase! The suitcase doesn't matter. He is going to die if he carries it; the extra effort will make him die. Why doesn't Mama understand? She can carry it if she wants it." We get to the main gates and see that we are to wait in the area right in front of it. A few people are there. Mama will go back for Daantje and I will wait with Papa.

---

[1] The shots were typhus injections, given to all those who could still walk.

8

ONE NIGHT: ONE DAY

Papa lies on the ground. I look to the left. Others are lying on the ground. To our back are the big barbed-wire main gates and far across the way is the Germans' barrack. Near there is a pit where big turnips are stored. I watch Papa. I don't talk to God anymore to ask that Papa doesn't die. I know he is going to die. I have one little carrot left. I believe that if only he will eat another mouthful of food, he will live a little longer. The sun is getting lower, soon it will get darker and colder. I say, "Here Papa, I have a carrot for you." Papa looks at me and smiles. His face shines and his eyes shine with his smile. His smile is for me. He says, "No, schatje,[1] you eat it, you eat it." No, no, I don't want to eat it. Oh, if only he eats the carrot, then he will stay alive! I can't say anything and Papa has closed his eyes again. He says nothing else. I eat up the carrot. I can't stay sitting with him. I walk around and around where Papa lies. I walk around and around him and cry without knowing that I'm crying.

A girl sits on the ground a little to my left. She looks at me and says, "Why are you crying, he's going to die anyway." Don't say it! Don't say it! After a while I can sit with Papa again. I can hold my body quiet and sit with him.

It slowly gets darker. From far across the sky I see a man run from the turnip pit. A German screams at him and chases him toward us. He clubs him and blood is pouring from his head. Oh God, they are running toward us. If they run here the German will see me and club me. If they

---

[1]*Schatje* is Dutch for "little darling."

run here, his blood will spurt and spill on me. He's almost here, I don't want his blood dripping on me. So close I hear the thudding of the club. The German screams and screams at the man. Suddenly the man veers off and runs faster. At the big gates of the next compound he climbs up and other men reach for him. The German is beating him. I don't watch anymore. The sky is darker. It gets very dark and much colder. Papa's eyes are closed. Is he sleeping? I sleep. When I wake up it's not yet daylight. I see the trucks have come. I see Mama and Daantje are here. I see Papa. Papa does not move, he does not answer. Papa is dead. I know, I know that Papa is dead.

We have to get on the truck. Quickly, already there are other people on the truck. Quickly, I'm so afraid I won't get on when Mama and Daantje are already on the truck. A man helps to lift me and Papa is put on the truck. Oh, maybe he is not . . . no, I know he is dead. The truck moves. The truck goes by the same road that we walked one and a half years ago. In shocked wonder I look out to see many, many wired-off compounds. To the left of the road and to the right of the road are compounds full of people. A few move around. I thought our compound was what this place was. I had no idea that we were a part of this endless, huge place! It makes me feel crazy to know suddenly that what I held in my head as our prison area, our compound, the only compound, is not what is really there. What I held in my head is not true, not how this place is.

9

THE TRAIN

The truck stops by the side of a railroad track. There is a small station house. We are hurried off the truck. Amid pushed, milling people we are to get on open freight cars. To each side of the railroad track I see a long wide trench. In the trench, on each side of the track I see chopped bodies lie. As if a giant hacked apart the bodies; arms, legs, torsos, heads are all jumbled, piled this way and that. My mind, my body are sliding apart. Chunks of my head feel broken off, falling, falling. I can't hold the inside of my head together. Inside me it's growing, filling up like a balloon without the outside skin of a balloon. I myself have to hold the exploding mass together. Like a mudslide that nothing can stop, my mind dribbles, cracks, bubbles out. I can't even think, "Oh God, my God, my God . . . help me. . . ."

Suddenly, I see two men who are clothed stand up out of the corpses, leap and run across the rail tracks to the other side of the railbed. The Germans shout. I see one man has a turnip under his arm. They run and fall. They get up, run and one goes down into the piled bodies. The other runs. I hope he gets away. The next instant he falls, shot. My mind is breaking. Then terror catches me. The train is starting to move! The sliding doors are already closing. Before my mind begins to work, my body is moving. I run, I run, leap, grab a bar and hang on the outside of the rail car as it begins to speed up. My mind says, "Don't be afraid, you can't be afraid because if you are afraid you'll let go and fall and be killed under the railroad car. As I think this, the sliding door is pushed open and a man reaches for me and pulls me in. To the side of him stands Mama and I recognize the look of utter relief on her face. I feel no surprise. I say, "Of course I'm here."

70

The train has many cars. The first car is painted white with a red cross. This is supposed to prevent the English or Americans from bombing the train. The people who could still walk are on this train. The others are left behind in Bergen-Belsen dead, or nearly dead. No one knows where the train goes; the grownups try to find out. I listen and try to understand myself where we go. Are we going east? "East" has a terrible, sinister ring. I know and I don't know that east means to be killed. Are they going to drive the train over a bombed-out bridge? Then we will be killed, drowned as the train falls into the water. Is it true one of our people talked to the train conductor and pleaded with him to run the train in the other direction? I don't know, I don't know anything.

The first few days I feel a terrible pain in my chest. I want to look at myself to see what is hurting. But I can't even move my arms. There is no room to pull away my clothes and look at myself to see what is hurting. The railroad car is dark, there is just the endless clackety-clack-clack, clackety-clack-clack. I must be sleeping in the same position I've been sitting in for so long. When I awaken I still haven't moved . . . there is no room to move. Sometime at night the train stops, we can open the sliding doors. We can get out and pee.

Day after day the train moves along. Sometimes we can keep the sliding doors open and I can look outside at the fields and the trees. I sit by Mama and I curse the German grass, the German sky, the German trees. I hear my voice curse on and on. Mama says, "But darling the trees didn't hurt you." I don't care, I hate them, I hate them. As I curse I feel the hurting emptiness of "Papa is dead." It is an aloneness beyond words. Now even the trees and this sky are not beautiful. This is German land and I hate.

While the train moves, the people who stay alive drop the dead bodies out onto the railbed. Isn't that what is dropping out through a back opening of the railroad car? I know that there are fewer people. I can look at my chest. No one pushes against me anymore. That was agony. Now I see I have another red and pussy infection place on my chest. So that's what hurts!

When the train stops, the German guards open the sliding doors but sometimes they don't open them. There are no Kapo here just the Germans. We need water. Where the train stops if there is a village or a house nearby, we plead for water. The people will not give us water. I forget food, I forget horror, I forget . . . only I know I want water. Finally, a few of us go into the house of a railroad gatekeeper. These people give us water to drink. The house has one room and I look up to see two pictures on the wall. The first picture is of Jesus. Blood drips from him. I know vaguely that this is the God of the Christians. Next to Jesus, I recognize the picture of Hitler. How can they have a picture of Hitler next to a picture of their God? But they give us water.

Now the train stops every day. Often there is a ridge, or hill or field closed off by shrubbery on the door side of the train. To cross the track I have to go under the train. Mostly I try to get water, sometimes we get some potatoes from village people. Each time I have to cross back under the train I am newly terrified. I think the Germans will start the train just as soon as I'm under it out of pure viciousness. They'll know when I'm crossing under and will get me.

One day of sunshine and blowing wind, the train is stopped because the first car was attacked by a bomber in spite of the Red Cross sign. Everyone who can move lies on the hilly edge of a big field. Mama and Daantje are not lying with me. I look over the field and suddenly think, "I could walk away! Maybe I could walk all the way back to Holland." But the next instant I feel Germany all around me—the hugeness of Germany—I would have to walk through Germany! Then I think, "I can't leave Mama and Daantje" but in a little corner of me I know that I'm terrified to think of walking through Germany, alone, hiding at day and walking at night.

Another stop brings us to the edge of a mine field. Someone of our people warns not to step away from the track. I'm afraid even to get off but of course I have to.

I am on the wrong side of the train. I have a tin bowl of water in my hand. Before I duck under the train, an open train bed of many cars comes clacking by on the next track over. I look up. The cars are filled with boys in uniform. I see they are very young; they are not men, they are boys. When they go by me they see my yellow star and curse me. They spit on me as the cars go by. I think, "Go ahead, spit, you are going to die. I hope you all get killed!" The bitter, vicious thoughts don't cover a tiny moment of surprise that even these boys on the way to the front hate me enough to spit and curse.

In a late afternoon, I am running along a bombed-out village street next to the train. I don't know how we got here, we are going back to the train. Two women I am with say, "You can rip the star off your coat." They have done it. I think to do it but it is so forbidden and so naked-strange that I can't do it myself. The thought even of taking the star off is too strange to hold in my mind.

There are bombing and shooting sounds in the far distance now, day after day. Listening to the grownups, I learn that our train is riding back and forth between the Russian, American, and English armies. The armies are closing in from all sides and the train is in the center space traveling back and forth to escape being caught by the armies. I listen to the grownups talk and can feel the edginess, the fear in people's voices as they talk about the Russian army. I don't understand; they sound as afraid as if it were Germans. The feeling I sense is so strong but I cannot understand it at all.

The train stands still this night. When I wake up, I look around and see only Mama, Daantje, and a man in our car. The sliding doors are wide open. It is quiet. Then, then a soldier on a horse comes riding by and yells, "Tovarich, tovarich!"[1] Soon after, as I look out the sliding doors, I see a group of Germans walking by the train. Their heads are down! They are tied one to the other with rope around each one's neck. Russian soldiers are moving them along. These were the Germans running the train. These were the Germans shooting. These were the Germans closing the sliding doors on the railroad cars. The strangest, strangest realization is that now they don't look dangerous. They don't look powerful. They look the opposite. They are like puppet soldiers without solid muscle strength. Almost I feel sorry they are being marched away. I really wish the Russians would kill them all right here in front of us!

---

[1] "Comrade, comrade!"

10

THE APRON

The gunfire has stopped. The train stands next to a dirt path. Mama and Daantje have gone ahead. I don't know how I came to be alone in the railroad car. The path is full of people walking, pushing in one direction. I walk with them. The path turns away from the railroad bed and still the stream of people flows on. The path becomes a village road. On each side of the road are houses and behind the houses, fields. As I'm pushed along suddenly I hear Mama call my name. She stands by a small shed. I move toward her, not even surprised that she is there, that I have not lost them. It's as if the moving stream and Mama standing there happened by itself, like magic. As I come to the doorway of the shed, I get a jagged flash of terrible pain in my head. Then the pain begins to push and pound. I cannot stand up anymore. There is a cot along one wall and across by the other wall, another cot. I lie on the cot and know nothing else.

When I open my eyes, there are some other people in the shed, talking with Mama. On my side there is an alcove in the wall where someone else is lying. Two men carry out this person, covered, so I cannot see her. She is dead. She had typhus. I have typhus. I listen and think they say that if the blotches on your body turn purple then you will absolutely surely die. I try to look at my arms but I can't tell anything. Mama puts the clothes we wore in a bucket on the stove at the far wall. She will boil the water and then the lice in our clothes will die.

She comes to my cot and says she has to cut off the rest of my hair because other wise we'll never get the lice out. I don't have the strength to cry. It was bad enough to get my hair chopped short like a boy but

74

now my head will be like all the other shaven heads. I haven't the strength to say anything. I live in a fever dream. I hear the pounding of marching soldiers and think are the Russians marching by? Are there always marching soldiers? Some time later, Mama says that the father of Bat Sheva and Moshe died of typhus. Everyone has typhus. I think bitterly that Bat Sheva's father lived through all this time, and now, now that we are liberated he dies!

One morning I open my eyes and go to move and cannot move my arm. I look down at my two arms and try again. I try to move my hand across the blanket. Nothing! I think to move my thumb, my fingers—nothing moves. I haven't the strength to move my fingers! For just an instant I am terrified but then I close my eyes. I haven't any more strength to be afraid.

When I'm aware again Mama tells me the war is over, finished! I lie, unmoving, on the cot. In my mind, I say, "I'm free, I'm free, I'm free!" Even the sound of marching feet that I keep hearing doesn't bother me right now. I only lie still, thinking over and over again, "I'm free, I'm free!"

I awaken. Outside the little shed the sun shines. Mama says I must be outside in the sun, that will be good for me. I move to stand up and totter for a moment, upright, before I come crashing down. Oh, God! Now what! I cannot stand up, I cannot move my legs, I cannot move. At all! So, another awfulness has happened? I won't be able to walk again? The thought flashes through my mind, "Of course, something else, terrible will happen, of course. Why did I think for a moment that this wouldn't be so? Of course!" But not to move? This is worse than even I imagined. . . .

Mama shoves me on a wheelbarrow. She gets the German boy of the farm family that owns the shed to help her. They wheel me to a green patch in back of the house and its garden. Mama spreads out a blanket and they lay me on the blanket. For a while it feels nice to be in the warm sun. I lie and see the grass, hear the insects drone. Later, I hear the German kids pass by the garden to play somewhere. It gets hot, the time passes slowly, it gets hotter. No one comes to get me. I try to move but I cannot. I can't even move to the edge of the blanket. Oh, I wish for some water to drink. Suddenly, thirst torments me. I cannot think or feel anything other than being hot, too hot and thirsty, thirsty. I shout for Mama to come get me but my voice doesn't make a loud enough noise. Mama doesn't hear me, Mama doesn't come. Some time later, the German boy comes down the side path again. I shout for him to get my Mama, to tell Mama I want water. He looks up but doesn't say anything. He doesn't come, he doesn't get Mama, no one brings me water. I am unable to move, I can only be hot and obsessed with water. I want water to drink.

At the end of the garden is another small house. Out of the second floor window a girl I barely recognize sticks her head out and talks to me. She says that when they can, her mother and she are going to go to Palestine. I listen to her and wish someone would know to tell me what we are going to do. To go to Palestine is the only thing I can imagine to want. Later in the afternoon Mama comes to get me with the wheelbarrow.

A few days later I can walk again. But now Mama and Daantje are sick. I need to get water for us. There is a bucket I take to the pump. The German boy comes to help me carry the bucket of water back to the shed. I want to carry it myself, "No, I can do it, I can do it," I insist. Mama says, "Let him help you!" No, I don't want him to know how weak I am, that it takes all my strength to carry the water bucket into the shed. I'm determined to do it myself. I have to go step by step. I can't walk in one motion. A step, stop, gather strength, a step . . . I do it. I feel myself half foolish. Why don't I let the German boy carry the bucket? But I can't. I have to try to do it myself. I talk with the little girl of the farm. I suppose she's my age. I tell her that I just had typhus and all the people have it. Most of them will die. I tell her it's just like the plague sicknesses people used to get long ago. She looks at me and doesn't say a word. I look at her and feel an unbridgeable chasm between us. Mama says to me, "Sanne, don't scare her with your stories." I think Mama is crazy. Why shouldn't I tell this child about typhus?

In the afternoon, a Russian woman doctor comes to the shed. She and I speak a broken German to each other. She tells two young men to carry Mama and Daantje away. I ask, "Where are you taking them? Where? You don't have to take them away!" She says, "We have a field hospital. We are gathering everyone we find with typhus so that we can take care of them. They should be quarantined to stop the typhus. Don't worry, we'll take care of them." I believe her just a little bit. Mostly, I watch and feel helpless as they carry Mama and Daantje out on stretchers. The Russian woman goes to talk to the farm family. She tells me they will give me food every day and I can stay in the little shed. Suddenly, she is gone and Mama and Daantje are taken away. I am alone.

The next days I have to go to the farmhouse and ask for the food. Nobody gives me food or tells me to come eat. I hate them. I think they should give me something to eat. They've had enough to eat all along, haven't they? When I go in they give me a plateful of food but I always have to ask. The room is full of people. One woman is nursing a baby.

I've never seen that before. I look carefully during the few moments I am inside waiting for my plate of food. I hate them. When the Russians came, they all hid in the cellar. Cowards! But they sent all their men to attack everyone else! Now they are afraid. Bah!

In another part of the farmhouse live two French ladies. They have come to the village with the Russian army. After a few days I go to live with them. They are fascinating. They look nice, they talk to me nicely. I sleep on a cot in a little hallway. At night lots of the Russian soldiers come to visit the two ladies. They talk a lot, someone plays accordion, they sing. It is noisy but a nice noise. I fall asleep hearing the good noise. The first evening with them they tell me they will have meat to eat. It is very important that I don't eat too much meat for the first time because if I do I'll be very sick. They tell me this and I listen to them. When we sit in the dining room, a real dining room with a big table and dishes, I eat the wonderful food and try not to eat too much. But in the night, I get terrible pains in my belly so I must have eaten too much anyway.

During the day they take me with them to find food. We go by a vegetable garden and we go in and cut some lettuce. They find other vegetables. They know what to get. The villager shouts at them and they shout back in French. My mind is watching us. I know we steal from the villager. I am happy to be with them and steal from a German. At the same moment, I feel guilty about stealing and afraid some German will come after us. The ladies aren't afraid at all. They laugh at me. I hate in myself the feeling of doing wrong. We should steal from the Germans. How can I feel it's wrong? How can I feel such nonsense?

A few days after, the ladies tell me they are going to leave because the Russian army is moving on. They are going with them and then one day they'll be able to get back to France. Oh, God! I don't want them to go away. Do they have to go? Oh yes, they are going. I feel sad, a gnawing disappointment creeps into all the empty spaces inside my body.

When I am alone again, I decide to find out where the field hospital is and visit Mama and Daantje. I follow a path that skirts some of the gardens behind the village houses and then veer through a small stand of forest. The path comes out in an open field and there at the edge is the field hospital. The woman doctor said no one can visit. They want the sick in quarantine. In the village I hear, too, that no one can visit. But I have to find a way to see Mama and Daantje.

I walk toward a long, low, wooden barrack. There is a gate in front and on one side another long wood building with open window spaces. That must be the hospital. In front I notice a Russian soldier patrolling.

His gun is slung on his back. He looks like a big boy. I lie in the grass so that he doesn't see me and take a long look at him. Suddenly, I come to a terrible realization. This boy soldier is blond and has a face that is similar to so many of the German soldiers. That type of face is recognizable to me. I think then . . . there must be others just like the Germans! I have a shocked awful feeling. This is something new I hadn't considered ever before. I think that always I'll have to watch out for and escape the "Aryan"-looking soldiers who will try to hurt me or kill me. The world must be full of soldiers like these! I am convinced that he will shoot if I try to get closer or get into the hospital. He walks from one end of the long barrack to the other end. When he fades away from me I squiggle closer. But then, the unexpected happens! The Russian woman doctor is walking with a nurse toward the hospital building. She beckons me and I go to her and say, "Can I see Mama, I really have to see Mama." She takes me in with her and then I see Mama in the bottom of a two-tier bunk and Daantje in the top. Daantje looks all right, he lies in bed but he looks and sounds all right. A pretty nurse is joking with him and when she meets me she jokes with me. She is Ukrainian and has a round face, black eyes, and red cheeks. I think she is beautiful and I call her "dark eyes" to myself. I am a little bit jealous that Daantje can lie in this nice bunk and be fed and have dark eyes look after him. Before I leave again, the doctor gives me the juice out of a big can of fruit. It is so sweet, oh it's wonderful! The doctor says I can come visit again. I just have to say that I've come to see her and they'll let me in.

It's almost evening when I walk back to the village. On my way, I see a Russian soldier beating a German man. It makes me happy to see it! If it were up to me, the Russians could take every German of the village and beat them. I feel that if any of the village people give me trouble, I'll go get a Russian and they'll just beat them up. I go back to the little shed pleased by this idea.

One afternoon the little German girl and I begin to play. I think of her as a little girl although she is probably my age, around nine and a half. She take me to her room and shows me a chest that is hers. I watch as she opens it. Inside are especially pretty dresses and lying on the very top is an apron. Immediately, I want this apron for my own. She takes it out and puts it on. Then she lets me put it on. "Give it to me, you have all these dresses. Let me have it." I try to convince her. She likes the apron, too. When it's clear that she won't give it to me, I take it. "I want it, you can give it to me." I quickly leave with this treasure and go to the shed. In the night I wake up. The moon is shining and I can see. I expect her to come after me to get her apron back. I climb up to the window ledge and sit there looking out into the night. I'm convinced she'll come after me and by sitting on the ledge, I can move in or out of the shed in a second. I stay there until daylight, holding the apron.

In the center of the village street is a gathering place with some stone steps to sit on. I meet a few other children there. I don't know any of them but they are from the train. One of the children is an Albanian girl. She comes from far away! She tells me that her grandmother explained to her that everything happens by fate. If you're in a building that's going to be bombed, then that's your fate. Whether you live or die is all fate. For some reason I get enraged at this idea. I argue with her, "No, that's not how it is at all!" We talk with each other in our made up garbled German. She doesn't change her mind and I won't believe her grandmother is right. From them I learn that on the other edge of the village all the orphan kids are living together. I'm tired of living alone. I'm going to find this place.

When I find the orphan place, it's a two-story house with a pretty garden. There is a kind of attic that we can sleep in. A young German woman and man live here. I don't think about whether they are mean or whether they are good. They have food and I can sleep there with a few other kids. But now, if I want to go to the field hospital it is much farther away. It takes me a long time to get there. I pass another shed where a few girls are living. They call hi to me and one of them knows me. She shows me that they pile blankets in a corner to make room but at night they spread them out so that they all have space in the little shed. I wish very, very much that I could live there with them. But I know I'm not big enough. They are old. I think maybe they are thirteen or fourteen.

One day I get an egg. I know that eggs make you strong. I'm going to take this egg to Mama. I start out, holding the egg in my hand. I walk carefully so that I won't break the egg by stumbling or falling. It is a long way and as I walk I get very hot and very tired. But I think about bringing the egg to Mama.

The hospital is so far away. I am walking forever in the hot sun, holding the egg. At last I come to the grass field and cross to the low barrack. There are no windows, just big openings in the wall. I find where Mama and Daantje are and stick in my head. "I brought an egg for you," I say when I see Mama. Her head looks like a death head. She sees me and says, "Oh, Sanne, I wish I was dead, I want to die!" I hear her words and look at the expression on her face. I cannot bear the words or her look. Hatred of her washes over me. Hatred etches itself into each groove and cavity of my body. Any anger, any hate I have felt toward her until now is nothing, nothing compared to what I feel now. God, oh, God, she wants to die and she lives. Papa, whom I wanted to live, is dead! God, I hate her. She doesn't care about the egg I brought her. She doesn't care!

I go to find the Russian doctor and the nurses I know. They teach me to say hello and good-bye in Russian and how to count to ten. The doctor gives me the sweet syrup from the fruit can again. The Russian army is moving on. They pass by; some ride horses, and some ride bicycles. The field hospital stays on.

When again I see the doctor I want to say hi. She is walking toward me and a nurse walks alongside her. The doctor reads a letter and makes a terrible crying, shouting noise. She puts her hands over her face. The nurse holds her shoulders and they walk by me. I think someone must have died. I wish I could see her face again. Two young nurses take me to their sleeping places and talk with me. They tell me something but I cannot understand. They and I cannot talk to each other in the garbled German the doctor and I use. It is not the same to be with them. It is as if a thick black veil has been lowered over the doctor and I cannot see through the veil, nor tear it away, nor walk around it to see her on the other side. I never talk with her again.

A few days later, I learn that I should come to the hospital because we are going to leave the Russian zone to go the English zone. I have to be there the next morning. A German boy who lives at the orphan's place will help me. There is one suitcase; he will put it on a wheelbarrow and walk with me to the hospital. I take the contents of the suitcase and repack it. I know this is what you do when you move on to a different place. When I see Mama I tell her I repacked and she looks at me with surprised eyes, "You didn't have to do that." I did have to do that, of course I did.

We climb into a big army truck and it is full of people but not crowded. There is plenty of space to sit. Some people are Dutch, one woman is French. She teaches us a song, "Dona nobis, pacem, pacem." It is Latin, not French and it means, "Give us peace, peace." It is a simple melody and some of us learn it and sing it in a round. I like to hear it and I like to sing it. The truck moves out slowly; the remaining Russians are moving on, I know. The village of Troibitz is left behind on this sun-filled spring day. Where we go, I do not know. The sun warms, there is space to sit, there is no terror. For the moment it is good, it is enough.

2

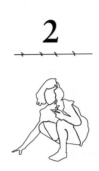

11

SHOCKWAVES

The roads are full of trucks, moving slowly. In the late afternoon we stop and go into a small building. People are there to ladle out food and we sleep in bunks. The next morning back into the truck. There is no end to this life on the back of a truck. We move, we stop, we get off, some others get on, we move again. Looking out I see trucks travel before us and some way behind us, and to the side trucks travel the opposite direction. We do not talk and no one sings anymore.

We come into a city. Mama knows of it. It is in the Russian zone and it is called Leipzig. For a few days we stay in a little room, sleep on regular cots. The room is in a huge building and there are people here from everywhere in Europe. All these people somehow have to get home to their own countries. Here Mama talks to a lot of other people and she tries to learn what happened to Oma. I talk with other kids. I hear the name "Auschwitz."

Unbelievably, I learn that there were many, many camps like Bergen-Belsen. I begin to hear names: Dachau, Buchenwald, Ravensbrück, and Auschwitz. Mama learns that Oma died in Auschwitz. There is something unbearably strange about the stories from Auschwitz. I hear as if in a dream. It is not a dream. Just like the butter story, what I hear now makes me feel crazy. Because I hear that there were camps even worse than Bergen-Belsen, I get a wave of crazy feeling washing over me. I've never before had the feeling of "crazy" but now I have to try hard, really hard, to know that I'm not crazy. I *am not* crazy!

Mama is upset all the time now. Sometimes I have to go away from her. Today Mama has gotten a cigarette. Cigarettes are just about the most valuable things the grownups can get. She smokes and lets me have a puff. I feel the magic. I want to feel the magic a cigarette has! A second later I'm coughing and choking to get my breath. What is this? Bah! The grownups can have it. I give the cigarette back to Mama without regret. Some time later, she gets angry at me and scolds, "You shameless little bitch!" But she says it in German and I feel doubly insulted. I have no idea why she is so angry with me. I go away from her, back outside.

Now we are on a train that is going to Holland. It is a real train, not freight cars. There are bunks on one wall to sleep on and seats and you can walk through the railroad car and you can look out of the windows! The people running the train are English. There is a doctor with a Red Cross armband. He looks at my arm. My arm has a big infected bulb in the crook and there are red streaks coming down my arm toward my hand. It hurts very much, but not as much as it did.

The doctor says he will make my arm better. He cleans it and does things to it and wraps it up with clean new bandages. But now it hurts much more than it did before, as if there is a little pump that cascades wave after wave of throbbing through my arm. I look at this doctor and try to hear and know that he is English. Part of my mind thinks maybe he is really an enemy and this is another way of killing me. Part of my mind watches and knows that that really is not so.

There are new things to eat on this train. There is soup from America. It is wonderful and awful at the same time. To have the soup is wonderful but it is so salty that my mouth and gums burn while I eat it. All the people in our section say how the soup burns their mouths.

When our train stands still and the train next to ours begins to move, I feel a moment of terror. It is only a little better when our train moves first, really moves, instead of only seeming to move. Every starting of the train makes my body remember the moving train, truck, or barrack move when I was desperate not to be left behind, alone. I look out of the window and hear the clickety-clacking of the train and see the utility poles whooshing by. A new thought comes to me. If I stick my head out of the train window, I can make it smash against a pole or another train. I can do it, not anyone else. Now, if I am to be killed, I would do it myself.

When we come into Holland, we come through the southernmost part. There is a big city here, Maastricht. It is very confusing to hear Dutch spoken all around and then something happens that is much, much more confusing. Some people on the train will go to Amsterdam. But I and Mama and Daantje and a very few others will not. We have to stay here, in Maastricht, because we have no "papers." We are stateless. We are taken to a building that looks like a school, partly. It is a convent and has a little outside garden space. This is a prison because we have to stay here, even though it doesn't look like a prison. In one big room there are cots to sleep on. There is nothing to do while we wait, day after day. But the most unbelievable and insulting fact of all is this; there are NSB families held prisoner here! The Dutch Nazis! I hardly talk to anyone. This is the most maddening, absurd happening. I go outside each day and feel my boredom. I cannot think anything clearly. It is so crazy and all I have to do is walk back and forth in the small outside space. I am so bored! Mama explains; to the Dutch, we are German nationals since Mama and Papa never became Dutch citizens. That was because they couldn't become Dutch citizens! But we are not citizens of Germany because the Germans long ago took away citizenship of all German Jews. I really think the whole grownup world is crazy, worthless, and contemptible.

Finally, I hear from Mama that in Amsterdam, some people from the Jewish community who have come back have spoken to the government about us. Soon we will be traveling on to Amsterdam.

12

WE HAVE COME BACK

It is late afternoon when the train pulls into the Central Station of Amsterdam. After a long wait, someone comes for us in a small open truck. We tumble on and Mama is muttering that it is *verschrikkelijk*[1] that no one was there to get us. As usual, I can't bear to hear her grumble and scold and I try to say that it really is all right: "Look we are on the truck now, aren't we? It's all right." When Mama scolds and grumbles my mind feels as if the "outside shell" that holds everything together is going to explode. My mind's "inside" grates as if the pieces are all broken up and put together again badly, without fitting just like the ice blocks that grind against each other in the spring breakup. I have to try to calm Mama or I'll really break into pieces myself.

We come to the Stadionkade, a pretty street of apartments on one side and a canal and sand flats on the other side. Vaguely, I remember that here lives one of the gentile families Mama and Papa knew "before." It is only a few streets down from where we used to live. The street door opens, I go up first, up a carpeted, steep, long staircase. I travel up on my hands and knees and the upstairs door opens. I see Mrs. V and hear myself cry out, "We've come back but Oma and Papa are dead." When I am aware again, I am in a bathtub of warm water with Mrs. V standing by the side. I am conscious for a few more moments and after that I know nothing any more.

When I wake up, I see that I'm in a bed with white, clean sheets. It is warm, soft, and comfortable. As my eyes open, Adrienne, who is my

---

[1]"Terrible."

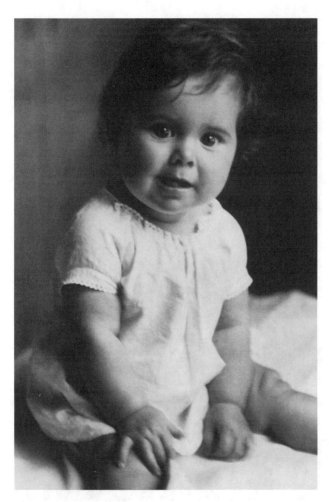

In Amsterdam, 1936.

With Oma (maternal grandmother), 1937.

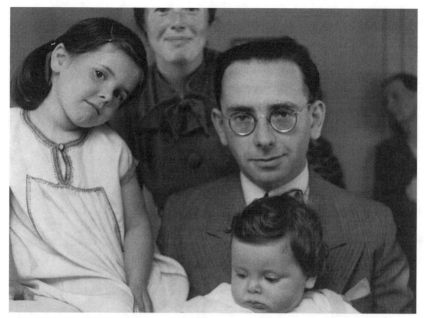

Mama, Papa, Daantje, and me with my paternal grandmother, Mientzjen Sax
Mehler, in background. This photo was taken on Shabbat. I'm happy to wear
my "Palestina" dress.

Daantje and me on the way to Copenhagen, Denmark, winter 1945–46. I'm
holding Daantje by the shoulders.

Home again in Amsterdam after a half year in Denmark with foster families, spring 1946.

My passport picture, 1947.
I thought, "Whatever
comes, I am determined to
be all right."

The first happy summer on the farm, 1947. Here I am in Tante Rena's vegetable garden.

The house on Eggleston in Chicago, 1948. For two days I could not stop crying.

Young adulthood, 1958. I
have a B.A. and am married.

Suzanne Mehler Whiteley, 1998. (Photo credit: Joyce Lopas)

age, opens the door to look at me and to say hello. I do remember that I played with her when I was little. I do remember that this is their attic room, one flight up from their apartment proper. I see Adrienne and hear her talk to me. I cannot say anything. It is as if my mind is a soft mushy substance that oozes out of its container. I cannot properly contain myself. I feel crazy as I look at Adrienne. Is it really possible that nothing changed here, Adrienne lived here at her home and at the same time we were in Bergen-Belsen?

The moment Adrienne closes the door, as she leaves, I stand up on the bed. There is a mirror hanging on the wall over the bed. Light from the dormer window opposite is cast off again by the mirror. I see a big head with a few tufts of hair and eyes I do not recognize. I pull at the hair but it does not grow longer. I look and see an ugly girl, such an ugly girl, in the mirror. I cannot look long and soon lie in the bed again. Somehow it is clear that I have slept into the afternoon of the day following our return. I feel utterly crazy. I can fit nothing together with anything else. The clean, white sheets, my unrecognizable ugly reflection, the light beams angling into the room, being alive here while Mama and Daantje are somewhere else with another family. I do not feel safe, or happy, or sad, or angry, or scared. I don't feel anything except crazy, edgy, not the boss of my own mind.

A very strange time follows. The V's are taking care of me. Mama and Daantje are staying with the Evers, another gentile family who were friends of Mama and Papa. I get a dress from Adrienne to wear. I also wear a pair of slippers. No one has extra shoes and in the stores there is nothing to buy. Adrienne has a group of kids in the neighborhood that she plays with. The first days, I also go down to the street. Sometimes Adrienne and I sit on the steps and talk. When we play with the others outside, I'm at a disadvantage slip-slopping in the slippers. The other girls all have shoes or sandals on. Besides, I discover that I cannot play with them because I cannot run around. I can walk but the group plays here and there, and so, often I stay to play by myself. I throw a tennis ball against the wall and to the count of ten do different tricks. There is a whole pattern that I learn from the other girls. I try to be with the others but when they move to another part of the street I get there long after they are doing something else.

Mrs. V tells me our old Montessori School will reopen as soon as they can clean it up and get the building working again. I learn that the last war winter in Amsterdam was terrible and that all of northern Holland suffered famine in the winter of 1944–45.

Then, in September when autumn has started we do begin our school. The teachers and headmaster take everyone out to the country to play. Someone explains to me that I will start in the primary room. In the Montessori School the first, second, and third graders learn together and children move through at their own pace. We begin to meet in a borrowed building still waiting for the school to be made ready. I understand that I sit with these young children because I do not remember much about reading or writing or arithmetic. But I am very unhappy and assure the teacher that as soon as we return to our school I should be with the other children my age. The next group is the fourth, fifth, and sixth grade group. There again everyone does the prescribed work at their own pace and I know I'll learn to read and write quickly!

While I live with the V's, Mama and Daantje are with the Evers family. Mama is in bed, sick, when I go to see her. I don't even want to see her. I feel angry when I see her lying in bed. But I know Mrs. Evers is taking care of her. Mr. and Mrs. Evers have two almost-grownup boys. Wilfred, the younger one, takes me outside to play and helps me ride a bicycle. He holds me and we start over and over again. I can really ride now even though the bicycle seems very big and heavy. Wilfred is nice, I love being with him but it doesn't happen as often as I wish. He isn't home so very often. Mr. Evers reads the newspapers and smokes his pipe; Mrs. Evers has a sweet, sweet face. When I am at their apartment I feel calm and easy.

At the V's, my feelings are more mixed up. Mr. V doesn't have that *gezellig*[2] quality the Evers have. It's not exactly clear whether I am friends with Adrienne or not. Sometimes yes, and sometimes no. I remember that when we were really little we played tag on the street. I chased her as she ran into the apartment stairwell, slamming the street door just as I was reaching for her. But it had a big glass panel and my hand and arm went through the panel, propelled by my eager chase of her. I had glass in my thumb and my wrist. Oma Deena came to take me to the doctor to fish out the glass slivers. But Oma wasn't comforting and I was scared and crying. I still have a scar on my thumb and on my wrist. Adrienne has her own best friends anyway. Mrs. V makes a dress for her and smocks the front panel. I watch her embroider. It looks hard. Mrs. V knows how to do many things, sew and cook and take care of Mr. V and Adrienne and me.

To my surprise, one day all the people are celebrating. I believe it's the queen's birthday, the first after the liberation. In the early evening, I

[2]Literally, "cozy." This Dutch word connotes a comfortable, pleasurable togetherness.

wander through the city. I've lost the others. I'm by myself but don't know how that happened. Everyone outside seems to be celebrating and for the first time I see fireworks in the sky. There are singing voices and shouting voices when the sky splashes a beautiful pattern of light down. Clearly, there is an excited joyousness but instead I feel more alone and lost than ever. I don't belong to this; not now. I don't belong to anything.

We are moving into an apartment on one of the older city streets, the P.C. Hooftstraat. Mama has found someone she used to know, Tante Kate, who hid in this apartment all through the war. You pull open the street door with a rope and go up one flight. There is a big back room, where Mama will live and a big front room where Tante Kate lives. In between is an "inside" room without windows. Tante Kate uses this room to sleep in. On the street front, off the hallway going up to the third floor apartment, is another very narrow room that will be for Daantje and me. In front of the big, high windows a street lamp burns all night. This building is almost on the corner and around the corner comes a streetcar and sometimes jeeps, driven by the Canadian soldiers who helped liberate Amsterdam. To the back, off the hallway, is a very narrow kitchen; it, too, has a very high window. On the same side as the stairs to the third floor is a toilet and another small space where Mama keeps a big round tin tub. Once a week there is hot water and Mama washes our clothes in the tub and after that Daantje gets washed and then I wash myself in the soapy water that is not hot but still warm.

In Mama's room is a round table where we eat. In the packages from America is chicken noodle soup. Daantje and I bargain with each other to trade so many spoonfuls of noodles for so many spoonfuls of soup. We do this every time we have the soup and enjoy the trading game every time we eat soup. One evening a week, Mama makes tea, and from the America package, takes a box of cookies. Mama, Daantje, and I play cards, drink tea, and eat cookies. I love that Mama does this with us. When I want to express affection for Mama, I call her "Mamuchka." That has become my special name for her. I think of her as an older sister.

When I awaken, my eyes are glued shut, this happens every morning. A thick goo encrusts my eyelids. I scratch at each eye until I can open them and then I scratch and pull on the lashes to get rid of the gook. Mama doesn't advise me not to do this. When she does notice my eyes she puts Vaseline on my eyelids but that doesn't make it any better. For more that a year I am in the habit of pulling at my eyelashes.

Now, when I lie in bed I can almost make myself believe that everything has been a terrible dream and I will awaken in my bed at home, as a little girl at home with Papa, Mama, Daantje, and Oma. I wish and pretend so hard that for a moment, it's the truth, all a dream. I'll open my eyes and . . . then the real truth comes at me and I feel worse than before the pretending. Now I lie in bed and I hear myself cry, "Papa, Papa, come back to me, I am so alone!" When I wake up in the morning I hear myself say, "Oma, Oma." I don't understand why I say her name because I don't know that I have memories of her. I just say her name and feel confused because it doesn't make sense to me to say her name.

Sometimes I get up from bed and go hiding in the hallway. I sneak up to the door of Mama's room to see if the light is on. I even open the door a tiny, tiny part of a centimeter to watch her. I hide in the little washroom to see if Mama will discover me. Sometimes I creep down the stairs, out the door, and into the street. No one discovers I'm gone. It's dark and cold outside so after a short time I return and go back to bed. It is important to be able to hide and sneak close to Mama's room without being discovered. At the same time I'm almost angry that she doesn't know I can creep out of the house and be outside!

Finally Daantje and I can go back to the Montessori School. We walk about half an hour to get there. He goes to the primary room and I can go to the fourth, fifth, sixth grade room. Our teacher is a young man with curly red hair, glasses, and a nice face. I don't put him into my category of crazy, stupid grownups. He is really fine. Slowly I get reacquainted with our school. Now there are books to read and boxes with graded assignments in the different subjects. There are puzzle boards to learn the geography of Holland and Europe. There is a wash/kitchen room off our class room and another small wing where we can paint or play a musical instrument. There is a bench built into the wall with cushions where you can lie down. The other person I notice is our headmaster, Mr. Eigenstein. I like him, too, but he is more strict than our teacher and some of the kids are a little afraid of him. Our own teacher has trouble sometimes making some of the boys work instead of fooling around.

I like our school because no one screams, no one hits, and it is a special feeling to be able to select what you will work on and then just do it. We ask our teacher to explain or check our work. Sometimes he is too busy and an older child can help you. I am like a wilted plant that now is being watered. I soak up learning. It is so good to do this. Now I don't feel angry at the idea of learning things—on the contrary!

There are about four other Jewish kids in my class. One of the boys plays violin. I like his eyes and he likes me. Once he invites me to come after school to his apartment. He plays his violin, I listen. I don't ask what happened to him during the war. I'm sure he was hidden. Another is a girl, much taller than I am, and she is the daughter of a man who was in Bergen-Belsen. I am jealous when I think about her because she was hidden and her father has come back. Another girl is beautiful and seems the smartest person in our class. She comes from Indonesia. She, her mother, and two other sisters were in a Japanese internment camp but it seems that everyone came back alive. I admire her and wish I could be as smart as she seems to be. When I visit her, the family shares an orange with me. It's the first one I've seen or heard of even. It is from Palestine, a Jaffa orange, so sweet and juicy! Another boy in our class is short, curly haired, with dark green sparkly eyes and he is funny. Our teacher has a hard time making him do any regular school work because he only wants to paint. In the back alcove he and his best friend, a Dutch boy, paint on boards with real oil paints. They paint trees, sky, the wind over water, and boats and all of it looks real and very excellent to me.

Even though our school has reopened it is not normal yet. We have very little paper so you write on both sides, edge to edge, carefully. There is very little coal, so mostly it is cold inside. I wear snow pants and two wool sweaters sent from America. For us, gum, also from America, is special and important to have just like cigarettes are for the grownups. But we have no gum. A few girls and I also start to chew our erasers so we can pretend that that's our gum. Our teacher looks totally disgusted and says not to do that. We think it's funny that he pulls such a face.

In our classroom is a black coal-burning stove. It stands on red tiles and in front of it sits a black iron fence that has a low, fret-worked door. For some weeks I go into our classroom every morning and hide myself by the side of the little furnace. Now our teacher has to find me, discover me. Then I come out and shake his hand to say, "Good morning, Mr. H." I don't know why I do this but it is important to hide and then be found by my teacher. Later on, I come into our room and go over to our teacher and shake his hand good morning like all the other children do. When we go home, we shake his hand good-bye. And down the stairs, down by the big main doors of our school, Mr. Eigenstein shakes hands good-bye with each one of us.

Mama has a radio in her room. Beautiful music comes out of it. Sometimes a voice speaks out of it. It is hard to understand how this can be. I know that there is not a person behind the radio because once I looked. Even as I looked I knew that that couldn't really be. But then, how does it work? I don't know anything about electricity and I've never heard of radio waves. I don't know so many things, but what is strange

91

is that I'm finding out from the other kids all the time about what I don't know. I don't know that there was a world war and that practically everybody fought in it. I don't know that on the other side of the world there was also world war and that another country besides Germany was so bad. It's so hard to find out about everything because I don't know what I'm missing. Money is strange; not the numbers of it. A hundred cents make one gulden, that's easy to know. But paying money for buying things is weird. When I go across the street to the grocer I buy cheese and pay the man money. He gives the cheese to me. Time is strange, too. I haven't known that you measure time by minutes and then an hour. The numbers are not the mystery but the idea of it is the mystery.

Slowly, most slowly, I learn that almost all people are not Jews. I learn that this is not the first time that Jews have had bad trouble. It is hard to understand because I can't think to make sense of it and nobody else seems to say anything sensible either. In Bergen-Belsen, some older people said, "It's God's punishment for our sins, that's what brought us here." When I heard that I thought about it some but I didn't believe it for a minute. God would have to be very evil for that to be true. Then I heard people say, "It's the Middle Ages again," and this began to have a most mysterious quality. When it was said the words meant much more than what the person actually said. But what was it all? What are the Middle Ages? What happened long ago that makes the grownups' voices so far off, remote, not talking about now?

At school it is easy enough to learn quickly. I work hard at the subjects. It is a great pleasure. But to learn what the people around me seem to know about naturally is much harder. I don't know how to do that. Every time I learn a new fact I have to rearrange what I've puzzled together so far. It is uncomfortable, maddening sometimes, to be so woozy about the world, inside my own head. Sometimes a girl at school will look at me, startled, that I don't know what she is talking about. Usually, they explain a little bit, mostly just enough for me to realize that here again there is a big empty space where I should be knowing something. Sometimes it feels very, very strange but I don't ever get the "crazy-going" feeling. So that's good!

On my way to and from school I pass a storefront where newsreel movies are shown. Today I see more than the usual little crowd of people. I push my way in, stand at the back and look at the newsreel. An officious, self-serious voice talks about a new bomb invented by the Americans. On the screen on the horizon a huge, puffy cloud grows and grows, higher and higher. The announcer calls it a mushroom cloud and says it can destroy the world. I move myself outside to the street. In shocked, frightened, doubting wonder I think to myself, "They couldn't, they couldn't! Grownups couldn't do this. Now, after everything else that has happened!" But then I think, "Oh, yes, they could do this monstrous thing; to invent a bomb to destroy everything." I walk away in a daze, overcome by fear and then anger. My anger is bitter, bitter anger that the grownup world can't let enough be enough. Now they've made something that can bring more horror to the world . . . to me? To Mama and Daantje? To my new friends, Charlotje and Elspeth? I thought the horror was finished with the end of the war. This bomb is a betrayal of my belief that horror has come to an end.

In the newsreels are pictured crowds of people. Another day I watch and see a crowd and among the people there is a man who looks just like Papa. When I'm back out on the street I begin to believe that Papa is not dead. I walk toward home and I believe it more and more. I'm sure that Papa has been looking for me, that he wants to find us. I'm so sure that I think when I come around the corner, just before our door, he will be there, waiting, and we will go upstairs together. I come around the corner, almost not breathing, and—and he is not there! He is not there! Knowing that I made the belief in my mind, and that he will not be there, that he is dead, knocks me almost breathless. Now the knowledge that Papa is dead comes at me in wave after wave of inside hurting. It is much worse than before I made the belief. The feeling is unbearable but I am confused also because I'm not completely sure that I was pretending or that he just didn't find us today.

Every week Mama gets a food package from the relatives in America. Today we have tea and cookies and a lady friend of Mama's comes to visit. I get presents; the most important ones are two books. One is from Mama and one is from our friend, Ilse, who also has come back from Bergen-Belsen. Mama says it is my birthday and today I am ten years old. She and the lady talk. I hear Mama say, "She saved my life." A murmuring conversation continues between them with "achs" and "ja, ja" interspersed. I have an immediate feeling of recognition of what Mama is talking about, but at the same time I am aware of turning away from that recognition. I don't know if I say out loud or only to myself, "No, no, I didn't do anything." It feels crucial to push out of my head the knowledge I surely do have that I took care of Mama. Because then I also have to know how often Mama didn't take care of me and that recognition is unbearable.

93

13

DENMARK

Mama has told us how she went to the mountains in Switzerland when she was a young girl. She lived with a family high up in the mountains and got very healthy there. Mama loved living there, better than living in Frankfurt where she grew up. One evening, after tea and cookies, Mama asks whether I wouldn't like to go to Switzerland. Unlike Holland, Switzerland has a lot of good food and Daantje and I would get strong and healthy there. It seems the Red Cross is sending children from Holland to other countries: Switzerland, Sweden, and Denmark to live with foster families to eat good food and get healthy. I don't want to go anywhere away but Mama sounds as if she wants us to go. So finally, I say that I would be willing to go to Switzerland but absolutely nowhere else. We don't talk about it anymore and I forget about it.

Then one evening in November 1945, Mama says that Daantje and I are going on a Red Cross transport. We are not going to Switzerland; we are going to Denmark. We leave tomorrow. I feel angry and betrayed. I don't *want* to go to Denmark. I *don't* want to leave my school again. The idea that I can refuse to go never, ever even enters my mind.

The following day Mama takes Daantje and me to the Central Railroad Station of Amsterdam. We get registered and each of us gets a card hung around our neck to say who we are and where we are from. It is crowded with other children and everything happens too fast for me to really know what is happening. Before we leave Mama says to me that I must look after Daantje, "Take care of him, promise you'll take care of him." I feel insulted. Really, doesn't Mama know that I would do that anyway? She doesn't have to say it to me.

94

The train is a regular one with compartments and sliding glass doors opening to the aisles. There are a few grownups from the Red Cross who will take us. But I have no idea where we are going. I don't even have a picture in my head of where Denmark is. All I know is that it isn't Switzerland, and I don't want to go but here we are already on our way!

As it turns out, the journey takes two full days on the train, a boat crossing, and two overnight stays in barracks on the German-Danish border. But I don't know this to start out. There are a lot of boys and girls in each compartment. Some kids climb to the luggage racks and use them as a sleeping place. That's all right until the emergency brake is thrown some hours after we are on our way. Everyone goes tumbling to one side. We seem to be cushioned by each other, though . . . no one gets hurt.

The train stops, goes slowly, goes out of the way because so much of the track is destroyed. I look around and see that I don't know any of the kids and so far I haven't noticed one other Jewish kid. Sometime later, we transfer to a bus and the bus travels through the dark, through Germany to the Danish border. I half lie on the back seat of the bus with another girl. When the bus stops German kids appear, begging for food. To my disgust the Red Cross lady gives sandwiches to the German kids. I sleep and when I wake I learn the kids had sandwiches. Now, none are left. Nobody woke me and they gave the rest of food to the German kids! I'm getting a bad, bad feeling about this trip. I go to the driver and all they have left to give me is a bottle of orange stuff to drink. I take a swallow and almost choke. It prickles and burns! What is this? Are they trying to kill me? No, no, it's an American drink and it's supposed to be prickly. I just never have had any so I don't know that it is all right.

When we come to the border, we stop and are taken to barracks to sleep. The barracks are full of three-tier bunks, lined against the walls by width and sticking out to the center by their length. I get a middle bunk. We don't undress and among a low murmur of voices I am about to fall asleep. In the instant I have fallen into sleep something yanks at my ankles and I am pulled to the foot of the bed. A man hits me on both sides of my face so hard that I am dazed for seconds. In sleep my mind is lost to me and for a moment I don't know what's happened. Then, I hear him walk up and down the barrack in the dark, hissing at kids, "Be quiet! Go to sleep!" Next to me someone said something and he thought it was me. Now I understand.

I sit at the edge of the bunk, reeling. I feel enormous rage and cast about desperately for how I can revenge myself on him. I can think of nothing I can do and that awareness enrages me all over again. But a feeling much more difficult to endure than rage now comes over me. Until now I have had two categories in my mind: the Germans—evil, atrocious—and all the other people—good, well-meaning. This man, a Red Cross worker, in charge of taking us to Denmark for good food, doesn't fit this neat division at all. Am I wrong then? Oh my God, are there other people who are vicious and unpredictable in their violence? It's too much to think about right now, but I resolve to sleep, curled up tightly on the far wall edge of the bunk, across the width, not the length, of the mattress. No one is pulling that on me again!

The following day, I try to find out how long we are to be here and why we are stopped here. We have to have a "health" examination. In another building we are lined up in a long line to wait, each in turn, for a doctor and nurse to look at us. I peer ahead and it seems that mostly they look at your face and throat. The longer I wait in this line, the more frantically frightened I become. Somehow, I have the confused idea in my mind that if they find something wrong, they'll cut my throat up and I can't tell what the exact "wrong" would be. I am half crazy with fear; and there is no way to run away. I get more and more afraid. Finally, there are only a few kids in front of me. A feeling of total fatalism comes over me. I almost leave myself and without saying the words my mind thinks, "I can't do anymore—it will be as it will be." It isn't the words I think—it's just a feeling I have known before. At night in Bergen-Belsen sometimes I closed my eyes not understanding if I would wake up and be alive the next morning. That feeling of "I can't do anything more" would come over me and I would fall asleep.

The doctor peers down my throat and I say ahh. Then he listens to my breathing and then, oh miracle! I am through! It's all right. The contrast between the terror I felt and the relief now makes me unknown to myself.

The second day we lay over here by the border, we are already talking and playing. At some point I and a bunch of others have climbed to the end top bunk and are fooling around until the moment the bunk sways in slow motion and the whole stupid thing comes falling down but not one of us is hurt. Later that same day another girl and I play with a Red Cross lady. She is young and seems nice. She lets us tell her what to do. We sit her in a straight-backed wooden chair and I start tying her to the chair. There is a rope and I go around and around with it and tell her she won't be let loose. We have a wonderful time playing this capture game and I really want never to let her loose.

Later, when the rain stops, we all spend some time outside but it's cold, puddly, and wet out there. Daantje falls down and comes to me crying. I see he has a little hole in his knee that is bleeding. I sh-sh-shush him. But I feel I must get help for him. The only Red Cross person around is a man sitting in a kind of caravan wooden wagon. A ladder leads up to him and from the distance he appears to me to be the man who hit me in the night. I'm really scared to go up the ladder steps because I think he'll knock me to the ground. On the other hand, I've left Daantje, crying, waiting for someone to look at his bleeding knee. I promised to get help for him. So I go up the ladder steps halfway, ready to retreat in an instant. I shout up, "My brother, my brother is hurt, he's bleeding." The man pays grudging attention to me and does not come down the ladder steps. I go back to Daantje. Later, someone does look at his knee and winds a bandage around it.

We leave again and come to a big boat we all have to get on. Apparently on the other side of the water, finally, will be Denmark. Then we'll go to Copenhagen where the foster families will meet us. It's cold and windy on the boat. Inside we sit around big tables and get bread to eat and milk to drink. But the surprise is that on each table is a dish full of sugar cubes. How delicious! I take some cubes for each of my pockets. Later, it gets windier, the boat goes up and down and it's like a shlup and surge, shlup and surge, sickening. I don't throw up but inside me the shlup and surge get me nauseous and dizzy. Yagh! Then, off the boat and back on a train. Probably, we'll never get to Copenhagen.

The train goes fast now, without stopping, and when it's dark outside we pull into a big railroad station. The Red Cross people say to get out here and we push out of the compartments, down the steep railroad steps onto the platform. Lots and lots of kids spill out, all with tags around their necks. It's almost too confusing to be frightening or to feel anything else. But really I'm very scared. And what's to happen now? A man and woman come over to me and the man says to come with him. I say, "Where is Daantje going?" He says another family is taking Daantje. I am appalled because it hadn't come to my mind that we wouldn't be together. Now, I already don't know where he is and I am being taken by the Mr. and Mrs. to go to their home.

Mr. and Mrs. are "Onkle Fred" and "Tante Lena" and we will go home to their apartment where there also lives a little dachshund. "Maybe I'll like that?" Onkle Fred talks German, which is good because we can understand each other, but is bad because it is German. In a taxi car we ride to their home. We go into a nice apartment. The first thing I notice is the little dog who barks and then runs away to hide under a chair in the living room. Onkle Fred is angry at the dog and rolls up a newspaper to go after him. I have an instant fellow feeling with the little dog and from then on a thorough mistrust of Onkle Fred. Tante Lena speaks only Danish but she seems sweet. I ask and ask about where Daantje is. Onkle Fred explains that he is with a family close by and that we can visit each other. I try to get him to promise me that tomorrow I can see Daantje. Finally, I go to sleep on a cot set up in a corner of the dining room. Next to the cot is a light and an easy chair. It looks comfortable. And so begin the next five months of our stay in Denmark.

The Red Cross people who brought us to Denmark sometimes plan outings for us Dutch kids. Once a week, I ride the streetcar to go to a downtown building where a group of us, girls only, practice singing Dutch songs. A few times we go to meet in a big, big room for dancing lessons. Once there is to be a huge party. Onkle and Tante come along because this is a Christmas party. A gigantic tree stands in the middle of a ballroom. There are mirrors and splendid lights all around the room. People sing and to piano playing we dance and run around the tree. We get candy and a little present. It's strange to be in a huge room, with such a mob of children, excited and noisy. I know this is supposed to be "special" but it isn't fun.

I have fun with the Dutch kids I get to know a little bit, especially Max. I tease him by chanting, "Maxi, maxi you've fallen under a taxi!" Max is my age and he lives with a family very near Daantje's family. Max's family has other children; he likes them and he seems happy here in Denmark. In Amsterdam he lives in the poor section of the city where we lived the four weeks before we were captured. He even knows the school because he's gone there. It sounds just the same; the headmaster beats the kids who get sent to his office. Max is tough and that's partly why we get along so well. We meet at the playground and stay to play and talk for hours. Max tells me about one of his older brothers who was in the underground and got caught by the Gestapo. Max describes his father who when drunk can "knock you from one side of the room to the other." Onkle Fred is often annoyed with me because I come home too late. Besides, he seems not to like Max. He doesn't like the other Dutch friend I make either. She is a little older than me and in her family there is a baby. She takes care of the baby but sometimes she can come out to play with us. She has "bold" eyes and is fresh according to Onkle Fred but that's exactly why I like her.

We all take the streetcar together to go to the Dutch-sponsored activities. Sometimes I can take Daantje. Someone on the streetcar asks how old Daantje is. I'm not sure she believes me when I say seven. She says he looks about four. We make a lot of giggly commotion on the streetcar. The Danish kids appear to be more quiet. In Dutch there is a special word for the noisy, naughty, disruptive fun kids have when they are around ten, eleven, or twelve. It's called "keet" and we make "keet!" But here in Denmark grownups don't seem to think this is okay. Another custom here is that when you say hello to a grownup, man or woman, you make a little curtsy as you shake hands. I want to object and I do. "In Holland, we'd never curtsy or bow to anyone!" I remark to Onkle Fred. But in the end I start, too, although I make the slightest, slightest curtsy as I greet friends and relatives of Onkle and Tante.

The singing group meets for weeks to rehearse the songs. I learn that in the end we are to sing on the radio as a way of saying thank you to the people of Denmark who have taken us in. On the day of the performance, Tante Lena helps me get dressed in a pretty green dress and brushes my hair and puts a ribbon around my hair. We go to the studio by streetcar and before we are scheduled to sing we meet for rehearsal once more. As one of the ladies leading us arranges us for a final check, she looks at me and says, "Oh, no, you cannot sing with this group, you are Jewish." She says something about only the kids from the Dutch Reform group are supposed to sing. That's everyone but me! Without thinking, I say, "Oh yes, yes I'm singing. I've come to all the rehearsals! Nobody told me I couldn't come!" I'm aware of how insistent I sound; I am *not* going to let her push me out. I love to sing. The lady telling me that I can't sing with the other kids gives me a tired, gray, twisting feeling inside. The real fun is spoiled and now I know again I'm not Dutch like the other kids. I'm just sort of part of the singing group but not really.

Nevertheless, the following day Onkle cuts out of the newspaper the photo of us, the "little Dutch girls," who graced the Danish airwaves with Dutch folksongs to thank our Danish hosts. Onkle Fred is pleased. He shows me the picture and says we should send it to Mama along with a letter from me. Onkle Fred thinks about me and does some nice things but every time we have a good happening, I find reason to be angry with him. The first week I came he told me that he wanted me to write a daily journal. I've never heard of such an idea. I don't want to do that. But Onkle insists. He shows me a book of blank pages that he got for me and shows me a cartoon cut out of the evening paper. It shows a girl and it says

"Susanne Scriver." It's the heading of a little column in the paper and it means "Suzanna writes." I give in and every evening I record what I did that day. Once in a while I'm surprised that I like to write in the journal. Mostly though, I make a very few short sentences! On the other hand, Onkle and Tante don't force me to go to school. There is a story behind this. I'm here in Copenhagen where I don't want to be, I'm already homesick for my school and being home with Mama. So on the way here I decided I wouldn't go to school; absolutely not. I think, "I'm not going to go to another school, I'm not going to be bullied by other grownups!" Onkle talks to my Mama by telephone. When I get to talk to her I ask her to tell him please that I don't have to go to school here. Apparently, in a subsequent telephone call we learn that Mama talked with the headmaster, who said I learned so much in the few months I was in Amsterdam that it won't hurt me if for a few months in Denmark I don't go to school.

Daantje isn't so far away from me. I can walk to where he lives. When I visit him, I see that his Onkle and Tante are very nice. They don't have children either but are younger than Onkle Fred and Tante Lena. Daantje has a little room with a table and chair just the right size for him. Next door his Onkle has a tailor shop and lots of suits are hanging on overhead wooden poles. Sometimes we play in the tailor shop. It's great for playing hide-and-seek and Onkle laughs and plays with us. I'm happy when I visit Daantje but I also boss him around. He hasn't learned to read yet so I think I should teach him the letters. Daantje doesn't want to pay much attention and he certainly doesn't seem to be learning anything. I get bossy mean. God, he can't just only play, can he? But always Tante comes and brings us milk and cookies and open-faced bread slices. Wonderful. On the way back from seeing Daantje, I go by the park where we play and near which Max also lives. Sometimes all three of us go together to play in the park.

Onkle Fred reads from a book about a girl my age who lives in Montana in "the West" of America. The book is in Danish and by and by I understand almost everything he reads. I like it very much that he reads to me. The whole story has a most mysterious feeling. I love the feeling I get from hearing or reading stories. Tante Lena cooks and I help sometimes, taking stems from berries or peas out of pods. Most of the food is wonderful. The most wonderful is when Onkle and Tante take me for a walk to a bakery and we buy sweet cakes. I get about three of them. It is almost unbelievable that anything can taste so wonderful.

Tante Lena is quiet and sweet. Of course, it takes some weeks before we can say much to each other because she speaks only Danish. Even though I don't go to school, I begin to learn Danish. When the children come home from school, I start meeting some on the street and we play. Onkle and Tante take me visiting on Sundays to Tante's relatives. It's a nice family we go to visit with lots of people. The ones that I notice are a big brother and a big sister and a little boy they call "lille Jahn." Sometimes the big kids take us out to a park to hurtle down the hills on a sled. They even pull "lille Jahn" and me behind them on the sled.

In the morning Tante and Onkle come to wake me to get up. This is the worst part of the day because when I wake up I'm so tired that I would give anything to be able to sleep longer. I can't explain to them how tired I feel. Onkle goes off to his photography store and Tante does some chores in the apartment and then we also go to the photography store because Tante works with Onkle there. I play in the store and sometimes outside. The store is on the ground floor of a big apartment block, facing a busy street. It is not far from where Onkle and Tante live. In the back is a little room with a very high ceiling and a door and steps to the outside. Sometimes I play "hanging" in this room. I play in my imagination; I will be hanged but somehow I contrive to escape. It is only at the very last moment that I escape and get away through the door. Even though I'm playing by myself, it feels like an exciting game. Later, when the children come home from school, I talk or we play for a while but then they have to go in to do their schoolwork. During the day Tante makes lunch at the store. Often she takes me home in the late afternoon to make supper before Onkle comes home.

One day Tante cooks something that tastes awful to me. It's a sweet red cabbage. But I don't like cooked food to be sweet at all! We sit and I can hardly swallow. Onkle says I have to finish everything. He is angry. But I feel awful, awful. Slowly, without deciding, I see that I am crying because tears drip off my face. Then I remember that today is the first night of Chanukah and Onkle doesn't celebrate Chanukah. There is no menorah and no candles lit or songs sung. Can it be just one year ago that Papa was still alive? I'm so alone! So alone! The food sits like wet clay in my stomach. I can't eat. I don't care what he does. I can't stop crying either. Finally, Tante helps me to go to bed and I sleep.

What Onkle and Tante celebrate is Christmas. Tante is knitting kneesocks with tassels for me. Onkle has taken Daantje and me to buy warm pants, a jacket, and ski shoes that lace up with hooks at the top. All the clothes I have are what Onkle and Tante have bought for me. Daantje gets new clothes, too. Some people we don't know pay for the clothes. I have a hat and mittens that Tante made. She can knit anything.

101

I look at her needles clicking so fast and in a few days there is another sock!

We go visiting Tante's relatives or they come to the apartment. The visits are fun but we always get to bed late. I get so tired that it begins to be like an agony not to be in bed, sleeping. I can't make anyone understand how tired I am. One Sunday I do get up early to help Tante peel potatoes for the coming company. Boy, there are a lot of potatoes! Before Christmas Onkle's store stays open into the evening and Tante helps him. We go to a restaurant to eat supper because now Tante hasn't time to cook a meal at home. It is so delicious! I get to choose a tart afterward, too.

We go to a big family party and it's nice to see "lille Jahn" and the big children. Everything is light inside. There are candles everywhere, even on the fir tree. I get some fine presents. A pencil holder and a drawing book and a necklace and a book called Uncle Tom's Cabin and a cutout paper doll and a little, tiny, tiny doll baby. Now there is a lot of visiting, and one evening the big kids take me out with them. On the street, they meet other friends and sing and laugh a lot. I'm so happy to be taken along with them but also I feel lost. I don't understand what they are talking about or laughing about or even exactly what we are doing out here in the streets. Later they bring me home and go out with their friends. The most fun is that there is a lot of snow now and during the day we can go sledding in the park. No one is in school right now. I and my Dutch friends, including the girl with the bold green eyes, go sledding on a steep hill down across the road. We steer the sled in a curve so that we don't crash into the apartment building wall, opposite. It's almost dangerous, which makes it even more fun.

Onkle and I don't get along. I feel angry with him a lot. He's too bossy! He doesn't understand anything! I'm reading Uncle Tom's Cabin. Everything I learn is new and the story of the slaves' life and Eliza's escape over the ice make me be far away in her world. I don't hear when someone calls me and when I do finally hear I can't bear to stop reading. Onkle gets mad when I don't hear them calling me. After I finish the book I tell Max about it and he wants to read it, too. So, I lend the book to him. A few days afterward I find out that Onkle thinks I'm irresponsible to lend someone my book and that he expects me to ask his permission first, anyway. Now, I'm outraged. Who does he think I am? If I want to do my friend a favor, I will. Whenever Onkle and I get angry, I feel he doesn't want me to visit Daantje as often as I want to. We end up talking about that. And this time too, I finally get permission to see Daantje every other day. But what I think is that Onkle is a bully and that's why I don't like him. I think he bullies Tante Lena, too. Maybe Onkle doesn't understand that I have very strong feelings about how things should be!

There is a holiday in Denmark when the children dress up and come around asking for pennies. When groups come to the store, Onkle doesn't give them money. I immediately think that if they ask for money they must be hungry and poor. So then I feel angry and disgusted that he doesn't give them money.

From Tante Lena, I get a few empty wooden spools. I tie a long rope through the spools and pull them after me as I go on the street. This, I pretend, is my dog. Mostly, what I play with this dog is being bossy, threatening to beat it to death if it doesn't move or stay still when I tell it to. I hear my mean threats and bullying voice and I don't understand why I play this way. And it's really fun to have this pretend dog; I take the wooden spools along with me everywhere and I call it Mollie.

But why doesn't Onkle Fred understand things? One cold Sunday he take me out walking to a big special park. He tells me to put on my hat and mittens. I argue with him that it is not so cold, I don't need them on! I can hear the exasperation as he tells me again to put on the mittens and hat. Doesn't he know how important it is not to get "soft"? I have to be able to be comfortable in the cold. I don't think about what it means but being "soft" feels very, very wrong. So we go to the park but again we are at odds.

A few weeks later, I meet a Dutch lady who lives in the same apartment block just down the street from us. She has lived in Denmark for many years. After talking with her a while she says I have a German accent to my Dutch. Oh! I don't want to hear that. I hope it isn't true. Nevertheless, this lady lends me a Dutch book to read. Soon, nothing exists for me except the world of the book. It's a story about two boys who fly around the world. They are best friends and repeatedly save each other from dire dangers. As soon as I start reading I no longer hear or see my present surroundings. I am deep in the exciting danger world of these two friends. I am them. This immersion goes on for about two weeks and Onkle gets most annoyed with me. Tante Lena doesn't seem to mind, though. She continues to be sweet and cook good things and start a warm bath for me sometimes. The bathroom is big! It's delicious and strange to enjoy the warm water and look around to the high-ceilinged bathroom, the far up window, and be alone in this big, big space. Of course, Tante Lena and I agreed I'm big enough to wash myself so she doesn't need to be in here with me. Still, she makes me feel cozy.

Some weeks after I get the wonderful book, I get sick with a cold. For many days I am really sick. Tante Lena makes me feel especially cozy. In fact, it is wonderful. During the day I lie in the big, soft bed of Tante Lena and Onkle Fred. A matchbox is a bed for my tiny doll and Tante gives me pieces of cloth so I can make a blanket and clothes for my little doll. This tiny, tiny doll gives me such a joyous feeling. It's like being in a dream world; I talk to my little doll, make her bed comfortable, give her food, hold her by me. In the dark bedroom softly lit by Tante's bedside lamp I lie, infused with happiness. Just from this little doll. How strange! It's especially important that the doll is so very tiny. Regular dolls I have never played with and haven't ever liked. This is so different. Then I sleep again. Wonderful.

After the new year comes, it gets cold and snows a lot. I play outside for hours. Often Max and I get Daantje and go walking to the playground park. One day we get taken to a manor house in the country. It is used as a famous school. Max, Daantje, some of my Danish friends, a Danish girl who lives in the manor house and two Danish boys I don't know, and I all go to play there. There is an attic that runs over the whole width of the house. What a great place to play! The boys try to lock the girls into the attic but we don't let them. We explore around and I come to a pantry room. On the shelf is a jar filled with thick, yellow-white syrup. I stick in my finger and taste a marvelous sweetness! After many, many tastings I finally can make myself leave but who knows what this wonderful stuff is? I've never tasted it before. Years later I understood that it was sweetened condensed milk I found in that jar.

Daantje and I get taken to see an American film. It's a first and stupendous fun. One film is a Mickey Mouse story. Another is about a small orphan girl who lives wherever she can be warm and find something to eat. Onkle and Tante take me to hear a music play called Hansel and Gretel. I know that story and in the darkened room the light is on the boy and girl, alone in the forest singing. It's a long play but I always like to hear music. Tante's relatives have a piano and I try to figure out the Dutch songs I know. I do, too—the "Wilhelmus" and "Mechieltje."[1] I love doing that and wherever we go to visit if the people have a piano I go straight to it and pingle with my right hand until I get the melody. It's not polite, apparently. Sometimes Onkle tells me to stop. The very best though is playing in the street for hours at a time. But sometimes, when

---

[1] "Wilhelmus" is the Dutch national anthem. "Mechieltje" is a well-known children's song.

I go over to Daantje and we play or when he comes over to me, I suddenly get so homesick.

Once Onkle said he would telephone Mama. That was when he told me I would have to go to school here. He talked to Mama and then I got to talk with her for just a minute. But she told Onkle that my school's headmaster said I didn't have to go to school here. After we hung up the phone, Onkle told me he'd been teasing. He really didn't mean that I had to go to school. I feel proud that Mr. Eigenstein agreed that I don't have to go to school. But much more than that, I feel such longing to be home in Amsterdam with Mama and my own school.

Sometimes Onkle asks me if I wouldn't like to stay in Copenhagen longer. Instead, I tell him that I have to go back to Mama and really have to go back to my own school. The first time I ask, it seems so far away that I almost forget about coming to the return time. But one day Onkle and Tante tell me it's only a few weeks before we Dutch children will be leaving. We go visiting again, to see the relatives and "lille Jahn" and the big children. I write in my daybook but now I am really not interested in telling my daybook anything, only that in so many days we'll be going home. With Onkle and Tante's help, I choose a present to take home to Mama. I select a sewing stand. Three sections open up by hinges when you lift the lid. Daantje brings Mama an ashtray with a picture of the Royal Palace in Copenhagen.

The train ride back to Holland doesn't frighten me. I sit in a compartment with two Jewish boys who teach me a card game. We play for hours. They tell each other Jewish jokes and that's more fun than the card games. I've never heard anyone tell jokes like this and they can both do it!

When Daantje and I come home to Amsterdam, everything at the apartment is as we left it. He and I share the little front bedroom as before. The street lamp outside gives a weak light if I sit by the window. I stay up reading my new books. When Mama comes to tell me to sleep I take a flashlight under the blanket to continue reading. The flashlight is made so that you push a small lever up and down, up and down, and then a light shows. The moment you stop pushing there is no light. It makes a zinging noise. In the first weeks, whenever we want Mama not to know what we are saying, Daantje and I talk Danish to each other. We laugh uproariously when we see Mama's puzzled face. Daantje talks Danish better than I do. I think he misses his Uncle and Auntie. I hardly think about Onkle and Tante. I know that I didn't take them into my head and imagination. I'm just so happy to be back home in Amsterdam.

Mama shows me the letters she got from Onkle Fred. In two of them he asked her if she would allow them to adopt me. He said they could give me good care and good schooling. Mama says she got a little frightened that maybe they wouldn't send me back to her. My God! I didn't know Onkle and Tante wanted to keep me. Oh, I am so happy to be here in Amsterdam. I feel as though I've almost had another narrow escape.

NOW THAT WE ARE HOME

Now that we're home again, I can settle into life at school and in the city with full attention! I have two best friends. Each is completely different from the other. Charlotje lives in one of the beautiful old houses on the other side of the city block where we live. The front windows of her apartment overlook the end part of the Vondel Park, which is in the center of our neighborhood. The park is big and beautiful with flower beds and play areas. Charlotje has a mama, papa, and two big, big brothers. When Mama learns about them she sometimes gives some of our bread rations coupons to them. The big boys are hungry all the time and can eat up a loaf of bread easily. Their family really can use the extra coupons whereas we get enough from the America packages.

What I love most about Charlotje is that she is full of mischievous ideas, and when we walk together to and from school we laugh and think up our next tricks. I learn from her how to have fun. We beg from pedestrians, "Could you give me a penny? I have only nine cents and need one more cent to take the streetcar home." When we have collected ten cents we go into a bakery on our way and get a sweet pastry. Charlotje can beg with a sincere, serious face. I mostly end up with an uncontrollable, nervous giggling. We ring doorbells of the apartments we pass, knowing the second and third floor housewives will come to the door and yell down, "Who is it?" We are long gone, giggling down the street.

As we walk down the street, I poke her upper arm every time I want to tell her something or get excited about something. She says not to do that. But I hardly notice doing it so how can I stop? One afternoon, Charlotje pokes me as she talks. Boy! That really hurts. No wonder she wants me to stop. Now that I realize what I'm doing, I can stop. We continue, good friends enjoying our way home on Amsterdam's streets.

At a certain time in spring, all the kids start playing marbles. She and I become marble fanatics. Our two-hour lunch time is supposed to get us home to eat and play at home with plenty of time to get back to school. Charlotje and I start playing marbles on our way home and sometimes take more than an hour to get there. Then follows a very quick swallowing of our open-faced bread slices before we make the return trip to school. It is approximately a half hour walk but on late days we run it in about fourteen minutes. One afternoon as we go careening up the stairs to our classroom on the second floor, Headmaster Eigenstein stands on the landing in front of us and says, "Easy, easy. You girls really must not be so late." This isn't the first time and after my shocked heart stops pounding I resolve to watch our time more carefully tomorrow, but tomorrow at noon we once more take up our marble play.

My other best friend, Elsje, is an only child. She has come back to Amsterdam with her parents from Indonesia. During the war they were prisoners in a Japanese camp. She has very blond hair and light brown skin. She looks pretty to me. She also lives in a big apartment building overlooking a large open area. Her bedroom is in the attic, looking out the front. Behind the bedroom is open attic space where her mother hangs laundry to dry on the wooden poles that span across the attic. It's a great place to play! We lean out of her window and dump water down, hoping to hit a pedestrian. Elsje tells me that a young man lives in the next room over. This knowledge is a mystery and makes us both curious, and it becomes important to get a look at this person. I climb out of her window and carefully edge myself along the ledge that runs along the front. Far down below are the pedestrians. Peeking in I cannot see anyone inside the little attic room. Gingerly I slide back into Elsje's room. We give up our quest for contact and continue other amusements. In a moment of passionate chase in the attic I yell out some street words to Elsje before we again giggle our way back to the room. Her mother admonishes me not to use such bad language. A few days before this, I sat in the living room with Elsje's mother, waiting for Elsje to come down. Then her mother turned to me and said, "Mr. P and I are so happy you and Els are friends. She is so shy and quiet . . . maybe some of your liveliness will rub off on her."

No one has ever spoken to me like this and I realize I don't think Elsje is shy. We've just become friends. I don't know why we've become friends. I stay overnight a few times, and the best talking we do is before we go to sleep. One night Elsje starts to tell me about the Japanese camp she was in. Out of jealousy and maybe despair, I don't listen to her. I say to her, "But you all came back, not everybody died. No matter how bad it was it wasn't like Bergen-Belsen." Neither one of us knows how to talk to each other about our life. We become quiet. We cannot help each other. What we are is friends. We like each other.

Charlotje and I learn that near us is a big, indoor municipal swimming pool. We go there and I decide to learn swimming. No one now forbids me to swim here because I am Jewish. It feels like a special bonus—a treat. We start to go early in the morning before school. Sometimes we go during our two-hour lunch break. Then we get dressed in just enough time to wolf down the bread we bring with us and run back to school. I love being in the water from the start and reassure Mama, "No, no, it isn't too much to go every day." Mama comes with me once and arranges for me to have swimming lessons.

The formal lessons consist of me lying on a bench and a teacher showing me the motions of the breaststroke, both arms and legs. After practicing on the bench, I go to the pool to be shown the next part of the lesson. On the side of the pool, traveling the deep length of the pool is a contraption that works like a pulley. Your "lesson" is to get into the attached harness after which you get hung into the water. As the pulley moves the harness, you are supposed to make the right motions with your arms and legs. One lesson equals a ride up and a ride back along the pool's length. That's it. It's obvious that I'm going to have to do something because I certainly won't learn swimming by hanging in the water! So in the shallow end I watch other people and start the swimming motions. One day I lie in the water and make one stroke to catch the side of the pool. Now I have my plan. Every day I'll try to take one step farther from the wall and "swim" to catch the pool's side. Soon I can go to the middle and swim back to the side. Then, the big test I set for myself is to go across the width without stopping until I grasp the other side. After I can manage this, my progress is rapid. The formal end of the lessons is that with a teacher watching, you have to jump into the deep end and come up to swim down to the shallow end of the pool. I stand by the pool's edge. I thought I could jump but I'm too scared. Over and over I think to try and then back off. Finally, the teacher gives me a shove and for the first time I'm in the deep without the harness! The first second's panic is displaced by amazement that indeed I've popped up to the surface and all I have to do now is swim. However, when I visit the V's and they take me along with Adrienne on an outing to swim in a river and picnic by its side, I refuse to go into the water. I have no confidence yet that I can swim in this flowing water and no intention to do something that will make me feel scared. I can't bear to feel frightened and stick to my opinion, although the V's try to coax me to go in the water.

One day I go to the big pool and see that children and grownups sit on benches on the side of the pool. Instead of everyone doing as they please, we are told to swim from one end of the pool to the other in small groups. As I swim I begin to hear shouts and cheering. I look around and suddenly understand that this is a contest and that I am going to reach the end first. I swim with all my might and strength and indeed "win." It is jarring again to realize I don't understand what is happening; don't know what is expected of me.

During August, when we have our long school vacation, Mama takes Daantje and me to the country. She rents a little one-room house that belongs to a farm family. The little house has everything we need: cots, table, chairs, dishes, and food we can get from the farmer—milk, bread, berries, potatoes, and vegetables. The farm family has a girl and a boy. Mieke is the girl and we soon get to know each other. Her brother has nothing to do with us.

I like being in the country but I miss Amsterdam. Mama and I don't get along. She gets angry but I seldom know why she is angry with me. Once in a great while she tries to spank me and I feel utterly insulted. But I also feel how absurd this is. Doesn't she understand that she'd have to half kill me before I would be physically hurt? At the same time I don't understand what happens to me at all. When she starts scolding at me my heart starts pounding as if I am afraid. Yet I'm not afraid of her. Would it make any sense to be afraid of her? What can she possibly do to me? I hate how I feel around her and I hate not understanding why I feel as I do. Sometimes I just leave and stay outside for hours. Once, in Amsterdam in spring when it was still cold outside, I just walked out of the apartment without saying anything. I was out for hours but it felt strange. I was out, not to play and have fun, but because I wanted to be away from her.

Annie from Mama's corset shop and Annie's sister come out to the little cottage to visit us. During the day the two sisters take me to a beautiful outdoor swimming place. It is a large pond set in the forest with a little house to change clothes in and showers to wash under. The water of the pond and the water of the shower are cold. Nevertheless this place is a wonderful discovery. There are just a few people there when we come to swim. We walk down the lane from our cottage through a corner where there are two farmhouses. Beyond these the lane continues, shadowed by poplar trees on either side. Next to the lane are fields and chestnut trees, orchards of apples and pears. We have to walk about an hour straight along this lane. Then the swimming pond appears off to one side. It is very easy to find.

After Annie and her sister return to Amsterdam for their work, I go almost every day to the swim place. Sometimes Mieke goes with me. Often I go by myself. There are trees to climb on the way. Once I find a tree I can really climb up into, high, far above the fields. I see church steeples in the distance and the scattered farmsteads. The wind rushes through the trees, rustling leaves and whooshing through branches. I want to stay up here a long, long time. The slight spookiness I feel walking alone along the lane is almost delicious.

The evenings are long, twilight-lit delights. A group of boys and girls regularly gather together in the corner of one of the farm fields. They are all kids from the surrounding farms. Mieke takes me. Most of them are just a little bit older but not enough to count. They tease each other a lot and I come in for a full portion! As an outsider, it becomes clear that soon I'll be in a fight. I know it is a test of a "snot-nosed city kid."

When the fight comes it is with a boy and it's over in minutes. I know something about myself that they don't know; I fight well because I don't care if I get hurt. I fight to win, not to protect myself. I also have found out that I'm quick; the fraction of a second that the other kid might hesitate, I've made my move. I like to fight!

After my place in the group is settled, they treat me differently. I'm accepted—the talking goes on unhindered and uncensored in my presence. These kids are talking about men and women *neuken*.[1] Amid stops and starts, giggles and silences, they are telling me some tale about what a boy and girl can do together. I truly believe they are putting me on; they're giving me some made-up story because I'm younger and from the city. I don't believe a word. They can talk high and low, around and through me, but I stick to what I think. Those evenings are mysterious and wonderful fun. I miss them when I return to Amsterdam.

Back home I find a postcard from one of the teachers. She asks if I and a few friends, Charlotje included, could come to school a day early to help get the classrooms ready. I feel really happy to get this postcard to be asked to come help at school.

---

[1] "F——g."

When winter comes we take pieces of cardboard and use them to slide down the snowy sides of abandoned bunkers that were built in the open space by Elsje's apartment. This is not Copenhagen! There are no other hills to slide down on here in Amsterdam.

But this winter of 1946–47 is unusually cold. The ice on the canals holds and to our joy we can skate and skate and skate! At school, we are let out an extra afternoon so that we can take advantage of the ice. I skate alone and I skate with Elsje. We can go from a pond in the park to another pond to another. Or if we start on one canal we can continue on another, going under the spooky connecting bridges. I have a pair of old-fashioned Dutch skates. The metal blade is set into a wooden runner. You bind the skate to your shoe in two places, as tight as you can. The bindings are woven of orange, green, yellow, and white threads. But the predominant color is orange, the color of Holland.[2] The ice is full of grownups and children. A few do twirly tricks on their skates but I try to swoosh and glide, smooth and fast, as far as I can.

There is a coal strike this winter, too. Often it feels warmer to be outside than inside, either at school or at home. In the morning when I have to get dressed, I take all my clothes under the blanket. I try to dress in the warm pocket of air under my blanket. Everyday I wear snow pants, the ski boots from Denmark, and two woolen sweaters. Once I have these clothes on, I am warm enough.

Since coming back from Denmark, Daantje and I spend our free Wednesday afternoon together in a special way.[3] At lunch, eating a thick slice of bread, we leave the house. Then we get on one of the streetcar lines and ride it to the very end of the line. Daantje loves standing near the conductor and riding on the tram! When we get off we have no idea where we are. Now, the exciting fun is that I have to find my way back home. We take all afternoon wandering around before we get back. Mama's only requirement is that I get us back before dark. Well, once in a while it <u>is</u> dark before we get home but that's all right. We wander through different parts of Amsterdam. When a few times I realize I recognize where we are because we've been here before, I feel a special excitement. Daantje is no trouble at all; he sticks by me like glue! After a while this is like a ritual for us and we never miss a Wednesday.

---

[2]Orange is the color of the royal family, i.e., "the prince of orange." The color is also symbolic of Dutch independence.

[3]The school schedule was Monday through Saturday with Wednesday and Saturday afternoons free.

On one of our journeys we end up in the harbor area along a wide waterway. A bunch of boys and girls are playing. The ice is breaking into big ice floes moving up and down in slow motion. One or two of the boys jump down onto the ice. The game is to leap to the next floe the minute yours starts sinking. I immediately remember *Uncle Tom's Cabin* and Eliza's flight over the ice. Oh, I have to try this. Of course one part of me understands that this is dangerous. The danger just doesn't apply to me. But I take Daantje and sit him on one of the pilings. In my sternest, older sister voice I say, "YOU stay here, don't move! I'll kill you if you move! Stay here until I come back to get you." Off I jump. From one ice floe to the other. A couple of the boys and I jump while on the shore the other kids watch and alternately cheer or say how their fathers would kill them if they caught them doing this. Having proven to myself that Eliza could have escaped jumping from floe to floe, I climb again up to the embankment, collect Daantje and on we go, meandering home.

Another afternoon finds us walking along one of the innumerable *slooten*.[4] We follow it, thinking it will eventually lead to a beginning of a street. In the distance I see the houses of the city and the many steeples that you can see from far away. The whole wide Dutch sky hangs over the field where we are and over the city in the distance. The wind blows; always it blows and makes the clouds move fast across the sky. The water, wherever you see it, ripples and reflects the traveling clouds. Grass, water, trees, and light dance and weave to delight my eyes, my wide open eyes as we walk along the path under the scudding sky.

Around Purim, Daantje and I are invited to a party by a lady Mama knows. Since we have to go in a costume I dress like a boy and Daantje dresses like a girl. When we arrive we go upstairs to her apartment to join a small group of children. This feels different than school or the little parties in Denmark. These are children we know or at least have seen before and they are Jewish. It's really nice to be here and then the lady asks me a question. "Nu,[5] Sanne, how are you doing in school?" I'm taken aback and hardly know what to say because no one ever asks me how I'm doing in school. I'm doing fine; what else? But I say, "Fine, I'm doing fine." At that moment I realize that this lady is the same woman who gathered us around an outdoor wooden table in Bergen-Belsen to try to teach us math. She only knows me from the time when I ran away and didn't want to have anything to do with learning math. How very

---

[4]*Slooten* are ditches that crisscross the Dutch landscape.

[5]"Nu" is Yiddish for "now" or "so."

strange. Doesn't she realize that how I was then, there, has nothing to do with how I am now, here. Grownups are beyond understanding.

In Mama's room, on the mantelpiece, Mama stands two identical vases of a smoky gray-pink-blue glass. In these she keeps fresh flowers. Today, as we sit at the round table for breakfast, I see that Mama is lighting two candles sitting in little glass jars, next to the vases. These are lit for Papa and Oma; they are *jahrzeit* candles.[6] When I get to school I choose to work on language lessons. I write and do the exercises given on the cards in my box; this box is the work for my level right now. I work and work, harder and faster than ever before. Surprised, I see big, wet drops on my paper. Frantically, I continue to work. Mr. H comes over to me and says, "Sanne, come sit on the bench for a while." He and I walk to the alcove where the place to rest is and I notice I'm crying, crying. I didn't know I was crying. Only I seemed possessed with a need to work, work, harder and harder, faster and faster. I don't stop crying, don't stop for a long time. Now I know I'm crying because Papa died just one year ago. It is his *jahrzeit*. It so happens that his birthday was also in May. I think he would have been thirty-six this month. Mr. H says to lie down for a while and when I close my eyes he goes back to the other children.

Just before this time, I hear that it will soon be Pesach. Mama says we will join other people to have a seder. I get a Hagaddah. Between a little help from Mama and my realizing that once upon a time I knew how to read the four questions in Hebrew, I prepare myself to ask the four questions.[7] We meet other people, grownups and a few children in a big room to have our seder. We know a few of the people here and many people seem to know us. At least, they call us the rabbi's children, the "Mehlertjes." I am both scared and proud to read the four questions. But this seder doesn't feel at all like ours at home did.

It is again a time when I feel desperately that I mustn't ever become like the "old" people. In my mind they are really most of the grownups. The "old" people talk and often their voices crack. They talk and have crying eyes. It's not exactly that they are crying. Talking and crying are each part of the other. The crying is in their talking voices. I've noticed this now so often. Each time it frightens me. It would be terrible to become like that. I must never, never allow that to happen to me. Never!

---

[6]*Jahrzeit* candles commemorate the annual anniversary of a loved one s death.

[7]The four questions elicit the retelling of the Passover story in response, but they also signify freedom: free people can ask questions; slaves cannot.

During a week when the rain pours all day and the days are gray and dark early, Mama says we'll get our pictures taken. The day before our appointment with the photographer, I begin itching all over my body. My hands and feet itch the worst and both begin to swell. I look at my skin and nothing shows that would explain the itching. When I stand up, the soles of my feet prickle and burn. We keep our date with the photographer, but walking the four blocks to the studio and climbing the two flights of stairs is an unbearable torment. Daantje and I are posed together for one photo and then each of us is snapped separately. While I'm having my picture taken alone I experience a strange new sensation. My mind feels the unreality of a picture taken that will show I exist. Just a short time ago I was so "almost dead" for such a long time. The picture taking makes my mind see, see backward to Bergen-Belsen.

After we walk home, my feet swell more and the itching gets worse. For two days I sit with my feet in a basin of cold water. I just sit and wait. I hope this horrible prickling will go away. The worst is that I itch from the inside, underneath my skin, not the outside like you do if a bug bites you. Thank God, though, it disappears all of a sudden without cause, just as it appeared suddenly, without cause. The photos come back. One is of a friendly smiling girl and boy. One is of a girl face that I don't recognize as myself. The face looks into a world beyond and I know immediately the photographer took it at the moment I had the strange unreal feeling.

One girl in my class has blue eyes and thin, white-blond hair. This girl fills me with an irritable, unreasoning anger. She doesn't do anything to me and yet I am filled with rage when I look at her. One afternoon, I make a sarcastic remark about her to the kids whose table I share. The next day, I also say mean things about her. To my surprise, the other children listen to me and I become aware of a subtle but shared feeling of hostility toward her. I had no idea that many of the girls consider me their friend and therefore would listen to what I say. The strangest sensation is that I'm utterly aware that I'm doing something evil; deliberately setting out to get the girl disliked and discredited. My sabotage of her goes on for a few days and then builds inevitably to a climax. It so happens that we walk in the same direction home from school. We yell insults at each other as we approach a crossing on one of Amsterdam Zuid's busiest streets. As we cross the street she turns toward me and without knowing who struck the first blow, we are fighting with full intent to slap, kick, and get the other down on the ground with maximum speed and strength.

Then she yells at me, "You dirty Jew" and I go berserk. Now, I want to kill her! As we fight, the busy grownup pedestrian and bicycle traffic swirls around us. Instead of verbal orders to stop fighting, now, some grownups physically pull us apart. They keep us apart and she goes toward her home and I, unappeased, continue on to mine. Did she ever make bad remarks about me before? I don't know. But I gave it to her good. She better not ever say anything else. Then, like a fire that flares up and dies down, my rage and dislike of her seem to disappear. Some weeks later we even walk home from school together in companionable calm.

Mama says she has something to tell me. We sit by the round table in her room. Soon the long twilight will begin. Mama says, "You are old enough to learn about your body and women and men." First, Mama tells me that soon my body will begin to change to get ready to be a woman's body. That's when I'll be able to have a baby. Once a month, inside me will wash away. I will know this because blood will come out. Then Mama says, "You will grow and sometimes you will feel moody and irritable. Don't worry about that." I look at her and my mind is blank.

As she continues talking, Mama explains that a man puts his penis into a woman. Grownups do this because it feels good and because that is how a baby begin to grow. In my mind, as she talks, I see the Kapo man lying on top of the woman on the wooden table outside our barrack. What Mama explains sounds too strange to be true but the picture is in my mind and I suddenly think, "That's what the country kids were talking about!" So it's true after all. I can't say anything to Mama because it's too strange to really think about yet. She says I should be sure to ask her if I have questions. I don't have questions though because my mind feels empty.

One evening Mama says to me, "They think you are very special at your school." I listen to her and feel happy that Mr. Eigenstein and my teacher, Mr. H., like me. Then Mama says, "I don't know what they are talking about, you don't seem so special to me." I don't understand what it is that makes me feel so bad, but I do. I feel awful after Mama says this to me.

In the spring, we get little notebooks in which we paste cute pictures of flowers and rosy-cheeked little children. Our friends write sayings and poems into our notebook and we each write in our friend's book. I give my book to Mama to write something for me. On the last page of my notebook she writes to me. On the top of the page she pastes a picture of

116

herself. Then she writes that I must never forget the great catastrophe that befell us. And I must always take care of my brother, Daantje. That is all she writes, nothing else.

I can hardly believe that this is what Mama wants to write for me. The thought that she believes I might not know or remember what has happened is so absurd that I cannot take her seriously. And yet. . . . It is hard to know why I feel so disappointed and so angry . . . but Mama wrote nothing to me! Nothing for me . . . I feel so alone, so completely alone. The pleasure and special value the little notebook disappears. Sometime later I lose it.

One evening Mama asks me a question. "Would you like to go to America? You know all the relatives are there, and you can go to school there." Mama explains, "Here you won't be able to go to an academic secondary school, even, because I won't have the money to pay for it. And what will happen if you want to study?"[8] I listen and feel a terrible pull, this way and that. Oh, I don't want to leave! I've just begun to feel at home again. I love my school, my best friends, and the city. I'm even beginning to feel truly Dutch. I don't want to leave. But what if I can't go to school? I've always thought that one day I'll go to "university" without knowing exactly what that means. Didn't Mama's young friend Annie from the corset shop say that I would probably become a professor and be so accomplished that she, Annie, wouldn't recognize me? I know it's true that Mama earns hardly any money while she works as an apprentice at the corset shop. Lots of our food comes from the packages the relatives send. All my clothes come from the American packages. But I don't, I don't want to leave. Sometimes I hear a grownup here and there mention, "America! The land paved with gold!" They say this laughingly but also with a seriousness. It seems they mean it. I think this is another piece of nonsense put out by grownups. I certainly don't believe a word of it. I feel resentful that anyone can even suggest a better land than Holland.

In spite of Mama's question to me, I understand that she has decided we will go to America. I don't know exactly how long we will still be here but the time here is even more precious than before.

Now the only place in the world where I would want to leave Holland for is Palestine. Sometimes I think that soon, when I'm a little

---

[8]After World War II, the Dutch voted in a government that mandated many changes. Among educational reforms was one that made it possible for children and young people to attend secondary schools and universities, regardless of ability to pay.

older, I will go there. But when Mama talked to me about going to America she said something else, very strange, to me. "Sanne, when we go to America we will not be Jews anymore; I will not light *jahrzeit* candles again. I will make sure that no such catastrophe will ever happen to you and Daantje again, or to your children or your children's children."

I look at Mama and don't know what to say. I don't understand her. How can I not be Jewish? I am. I feel a disquiet. An alarm that is not yet clanging, that cannot yet be expressed in words. I hope it will be a long time yet before we go to America.

One lunch time I come home, late as usual, to see a note to me from Mama stuck on the street door. It says, "I had to go to the consulate. I couldn't wait for you any longer." I don't have a key and I can't reach in through the mail slot to pull the rope that controls the door lock on the inside. I walk all the way around the city block to where Charlotje lives. When I go up the stairs there, I am surprised to notice I am crying and even more surprised to hear Charlotje's mother say, "Well, come up, come up, of course we'll give you a sandwich." I can't understand myself getting upset because Mama isn't there. I've been away from her so often. Why should I care that she isn't there this lunch time? Even though some of my mind knows it isn't true, another part of me thinks I'll never see her again.

The consulate is the American consulate, and some weeks later another requirement makes me realize that emigrating to America is really going to happen. We have to go to Rotterdam to get a health exam and to answer questions. We arrive, leave the train station, and come upon an open, wide plain. Once, before the German blitz, this was the center of Rotterdam; now you can see buildings only in the far distance. We go into one of these buildings, and each of us in turn is asked questions. An American lady asks me if I am looking forward to going to America. I say, "I don't want to go at all." She answers, "Oh, you'll love it there." We don't get a health exam exactly. Someone looks in our eyes and listens to our chest. I don't feel scared.

At school, my teacher and the children have learned that soon I'll be leaving for America. My best friends each give me a book. Another girl in my class, on the very last day, gives me a book with a good-bye note in it. I am so surprised. She is cute and has a younger sister, also in our class and cute, both of them with curly hair braids and blue eyes and laughing faces. But I didn't expect a present from them!

Another person tells Mama that she wants to give me a present. It is the lady who knows how to sew, a seamstress who made a dress for me from green velvet and pieces of red, white, and green checked cloth. One afternoon I walk to the apartment where she lives. It is a rainy day and now, after school, already getting dark. She lives in a basement apartment of one big room. She has a girl, too, I think. When I go into the room, she shows me a lovely bracelet made out of silver Dutch ten-cent pieces called *dubbeltjes*.[9] On the face of each coin is a picture of Queen Wilhelmina. The space around the face is cut out so each link has a delicate look. I know that this lady is really very poor. I know this just by walking into her room. I can sense her heart's feeling toward me, not only because of the bracelet but by the way she says good-bye to me.

The bracelet is especially Dutch. I treasure it. What a strange event! The seamstress lady, whom I hardly know, wanted to say good-bye to me, specially, and gave me this very wonderful present. I feel this as I walk home on the dark, glistening, wet streets. I also know again that soon we will really leave for America.

The sun is shining on the day we leave for America. We walk down the street, around the corner, to a taxi car that will drive us to the airport. We are going to fly in an airplane. We carry suitcases, no rucksacks. As we turn the corner, I am filled with numbing despair. Somehow it is clear to me that this time I will not "come back." The helplessness that pervades me is more vague and more overpowering than any I have felt before. I am eleven and a half but really I am seven going on seventy-nine. Like a seven-year-old I can barely keep track of the factual happenings of our lives. I barely manage some understanding of what is going on around me. Like a seventy-nine-year-old woman I feel old. Old and exhausted, so exhausted. I feel that there is nothing left to experience that can be "real." I think that nothing will feel as "real" as what has already happened.

It is May 1947, exactly seven years from that May of the invasion when I was four and a half.

---

[9]"Little doubles" means a ten-cent piece, double the five-cent coin.

3

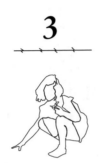

15

THE POINT

I am walking out on the "point," that circular outcropping of rocks and grassy park reaching into Lake Michigan. The neighborhood behind me surrounds the University of Chicago and is called Hyde Park. I live there, alone, in a rooming house, apart now from Mama, Daan, and Tante Lisel, Papa's sister. We've lived together seven years, ever since settling in Chicago in the fall of 1947. I glory in the solitude of my room, saying over and over again, "I'm alone, I'm alone!" A litany of joy expressing my relief at getting away from the constant quarreling between my mother and my aunt. I am in my third year at the University of Chicago, supposedly my last year, meeting the requirements for a B.A. in three years of intense study.

I feel no joy walking on these rocks. I intended to swim, sliding into the deep water off the "point" as I have done many a summer before, at home in the water like a seal. But my mind is doing strange things. I look at the signs painted on many of the rocks. "No swimming," they say. Signs I and others have always ignored now frighten me so much that I don't go into the water. I no longer control my mind. I remember that I used to swim here fearlessly. I know that I am the same person I was then but I can't find me. I am sliding out of reach. I can't study anymore, my mind won't concentrate, won't do the work I tell it to do. Oh, I go to class and I go to my job at the Faculty Club. There I serve lunch to the members and their guests who sit around big tables as we bring out their dishes on big, round trays. It is a good job because I get my meal of the day there and also thirty-some cents an hour. I've had part-time jobs since the summer I was thirteen but never before has my brain stopped working. I can't count on the one part of me that I have always been able to count on.

I've been waiting and hoping to feel grown up but instead I feel more and more lost. There is hardly any of the me I used to know left. I'm so scared. What is happening to me? I cry all the time. Crying like that makes me more scared. I don't know how to stop. I don't know how to live if now my brain is going to stop, too. Am I going crazy?

Once I saved myself from drowning. Knowingly, consciously, I saved myself from drowning in the North Sea. That cold sea that licks and laps the entire west coast of Holland. It licks and laps when quiet; when in storm it is a destroyer of the world. Behind the barrier dunes held down by tough, anchoring grasses sit the old fishing villages up and down the coast. For a few days in the summer of 1946, Tante Kate took me with her to vacation in one of these villages. Together we slept in a cold, small, attic room, its one small window looking out to sea. Aunt's harsh, rattling snores were so loud that it always surprised me that I had fallen asleep while trying not to listen to them. Nothing had yet been rebuilt or added to the old village since the war. It was a time of empty stretches of sand, with an occasional man or woman sitting in the large round-backed wicker chairs that protect the Dutch from the cold sea winds. Tante Kate sat and read, did not swim, but looked out on the open vista. I never asked her what it might be like to be in the open air after the years of hiding in her own apartment, imprisoned in the old-fashioned inner room of the nineteenth-century building she lived in. I didn't ask because I was unable to imagine anything bad happening to her in those long years. She was, after all, alive and had escaped Bergen-Belsen or Auschwitz. We had not much in common, not much to say to each other, but I did feel honored that she had invited me to go with her.

For me the sea was irresistible. Inured to cold, I was eager to use my new swimming skills and every day found me in the water. The immensity of the sea and the lack of people on the strand did not frighten me. I thrilled to experience my new skill. One moment I was swimming easily, happily, thinking to turn back toward the shore. The next moment I felt the tremendous surging of the water, the undertow pushing me away, out to sea. Seconds of panic as I felt my puniness against that power of the surf. Thoughts of horror, "I'm going to die after all." Then, as if my mind made an actual click, I thought, "Don't panic, all you have to do is not panic, just don't panic." Without more words, I knew that I had felt this once before, that I had thought like this once before. Because I had caught a familiar experience I could think my way out of danger.

Looking toward the beach I swam at a long diagonal. I don't know whether it was trial and error or whether I'd been told or read somewhere that to overcome the power of a current you must swim at an angle. I told myself that it would take a long time to swim back this way but I shouldn't be afraid. After many long minutes I saw myself getting closer to shore and knew the "stop panicking" impulse would get me safely back to land. Very tired and very shaken I came out of the water and never mentioned to anyone what had happened. The realization that I had known how to save myself was a secret I treasured.

So now how can I possibly make sense out of my fear? I do know that since I've come to live in America I have periodically lost my mind. Something will stir a memory or a feeling and I lose all sense of where I am and what is happening. Two years ago, my favorite professor had advised me to go to student health to talk to someone who might be able to help me. He spoke to me in his office after an incident in class which must have frightened my friends and onlookers even more than it frightened me.

In class we had looked at Picasso's painting *Guernica*. This painting was Picasso's response to the first bombing of civilians by the Germans in the Spanish Civil War of the 1930s. One young classmate said, "I don't see how this connects to the bombing or the war." I started to explain to him what I saw in the painting and as I heard my voice talking, I found myself holding on to the doorjamb, then falling to the floor. A voice was screaming. I heard the screams as I saw that I was lying in the hallway just outside the classroom. I still heard screams, then crying as my mind slowly came back to me. A friend from class stayed with me until I could stand up and speak. I went through the rest of the day's schedule as I always did. And as always it took many days for me to get rid of the shaking feeling that I experienced all through my body. It was after this episode that my teacher suggested I talk to someone. But the idea was utterly foreign to me and also scared me. I did nothing.

But now I can't go on like this. I cry more and more. If I can't study, I can't finish my degree. How will I take care of myself? How will I earn enough to live? If I can't study and have the joy of learning and the joy of ideas available to me, how can I go on?

What has happened in the past seven years that has brought me to this abyss? What must I do to save myself?

16

NEW YORK

According to geography our DC-6 has landed on a new continent. But to me it is like landing on a different planet. The trip itself seemed to go on forever, twelve hours of it or maybe more. The plane refueled in Ireland then in Newfoundland. There we waited, dozing on and off in big stuffed chairs while outside in a blowing snow-storm, the plane was checked over. On the plane, in front of each seat is a pocket containing a flight bag to throw up in if you get sick. I looked at the bag and determined I would not get sick. But during the last leg of the trip, flying from Newfoundland to New York, nausea overcame me.

Now we are waiting in line in a huge one-story building to be "cleared" through. Though I'm prepared to wait forever, we don't have to be in that building very long. When we come out Uncle Hans meets us. He takes us to walk through a few streets to his car, which will take us to where he lives.

It is mid-morning. On either side of the street the buildings are huge, tall blocks reaching into the sky. I don't see plazas or trees or waterways. I can hardly see the sky itself. My ears are assaulted by the English sound all around me. They throb, hearing but not able to sort out the thrumming noise into separate sounds. My ears are not used to hearing meaningless sound. I feel emptied out by the strangeness of it all.

Then we get to Uncle's house. I'm overwhelmed by the richness of it. In Holland a separate house with a garden is called a villa. I've never before been inside a villa and I don't know anyone else who has

126

either.[1] The house is very light inside and has four bedrooms upstairs. Downstairs from the kitchen is a room made out of part of the basement. Here on two cots Daantje and I will sleep. Off the side of the kitchen is a tiny bedroom with its own bathroom. Its bright window looks onto a red rosebush in the back garden. Here Mama will sleep.

The bright house is full of people. Uncle and Aunt, their two older girls, Rena a year older than I am and Ellen a year younger. There is a little girl with huge, dark eyes in a highchair; her name is Amy. There is also Tante Lily, who is Oma's sister. I look carefully at Tante Lily to see if there is anything about her that is like my Oma but I don't see any resemblance. The bright house has a richness of relatives!

It is not yet afternoon. All together nine people sit around the kitchen table and eat a meal. Now I realize the richness of America—food! After the meal Rena and Ellen have to return to school and excitedly ask that I come along. The grownups confer and I'm sent off with Rena to go to her class. We walk about two blocks onto a big play area and go into a cavernous building. Rena is in sixth grade. She walks up to her teacher to introduce me. I stick out my hand to shake his and say, "Dag Myneer."[2] Of course I don't understand one word the teacher says to me and have no idea what is going on in the class. By the end of the afternoon, though, I have learned to say and understand "yes" and "no."

The weeks that follow are a kaleidoscope of experiences. At the start I feel swamped by an auditory ocean of meaningless sound. After some days without my even trying I begin to hear some recognizable sounds. I hear the separate sounds without understanding any words yet. After a few weeks I begin to understand some of what people say around me although I can't say anything yet. In the classroom I still haven't any idea of what they are doing. The teacher allows me a corner of the blackboard where I draw an object and write the English name underneath. I draw things I've seen in a picture dictionary sent to us by the relatives. A few times Aunt sits with me after school and tries to help me say some English words. I can tell she is eager for me to learn but a strange indifference inhabits me. I feel no inner urgency and am a little puzzled by my own lassitude, so different from what I know of myself.

---

[1]After World War II and especially since the 1960s, there has been a great deal of construction of apartment blocks, townhouses, and freestanding houses to provide for a tremendous population increase. This statement no longer describes the housing situation.

[2]"Hello, Sir."

At the school the children line up to go into the school and class. At day's end they line up to leave the classroom to go home. Each time I break rank and walk over to the teacher to shake his hand and say "hello" or "good-bye." He looks at me strangely and then shakes my hand. I begin to know I won't do this forever, since here, in this New York school, the behavior is so different. Suddenly all my homesick longings for Amsterdam are bound up with not shaking hands. Each hello and good-bye sends an arrow of aching into my heart.

My cousins take me along to play after school in the school playground. I'm used to playing loud and rough with girls and boys. Here the rules are different; I can sense it without understanding what the rules are. Charlotje and I played *foetbal*[3] with the boys in our classes; here I don't play with the boys. One afternoon at home Rena is crying and saying to her mother that I play wrong with the boys. Rena is embarrassed. I'm uneasy that she's crying about something to do with me. But I don't know what I'm doing wrong. Slowly I lose the feeling of knowing how to act. Knowing automatically without having to think about it.

In the afternoon we stay around school for activities. I learn about baseball; girls play softball. It's such a slow game that I don't understand why the kids like to play it. Inside the school building the gym teacher puts on a record and teaches us a "square" dance. The kids seem not to like this much but I like it. The music sounds strange but fun. One afternoon the classes go to the auditorium on the third floor to be shown a movie. I sit next to Rena. The big high-ceilinged room is darkened and the movie starts. It is something about war with the Japanese. I don't understand what I am seeing or what I am hearing until suddenly the screen is full of men prisoners fighting for bowls of soup. They shove and claw at each other in desperation. As if I'm there, with them, my heart pounds, sickness fills my stomach, my mind is breaking. I don't know whether I am falling or crying or moaning but when I become aware again I'm walking down the stairs with a teacher and Rena holding me on each side. Someone telephones Mama and when she comes the teacher says she'll drive us home. Mama says, "That is not necessary, we are so close to the school." The teacher insists. I get in the back of the car, Mama sits in front with the teacher and they talk. "Did she see some of those terrible things?" the teacher asks. "Yes, of course," Mama answers. "You don't mind my asking? She can't understand us anyway."

---

[3]*Foetbal* is Dutch for "soccer."

I listen, understanding very well although I can't say anything yet in English. A familiar feeling goes through me. Stupid grownups! Here's another one. Doesn't she know that by this time I do understand simple English? Doesn't she know that first you learn to understand and then slowly you learn to speak?

I feel horrible. There is a sick aftershaking in my body. I don't understand what happened to me and I know nothing shows on the outside. That feeling of my mind going dark is more than scary. The entire inside hollow of my body feels bad. I wish I could stop it all. All feeling, all thinking.

The next afternoon during activities time I overhear one teacher say to another, "I don't understand how she can laugh and play today when she was so upset yesterday." They think I don't know that they are talking about me. They don't know that you can be screaming one moment but then it stops. Just because you cry doesn't mean you cry twenty-four hours, does it? I'm troubled. It sounds to me as if they disapprove. At Uncle and Aunt's house also no one understands. I sense that everyone is pleased to see my playing, laughing. No one asks or comments on the past. No one wants to know anything. I don't know how I learn this but it is very, very clear. No one wants to know and no one wants to hear about what has happened in Europe.

Each supper time I revel in the delicious food. Usually I eat one more helping, one more potato, and one more. Great Aunt Lily says, "Don't let the child eat another one, she'll be sick." Sick?! She doesn't know anything either, about being hungry or the wonder of food, enough food! When the carrots or potatoes are peeled I look at the peelings and think, "That would still make a meal." When the dishes are taken to the sink, I look at the scraps and leftovers and think, "Ja, that would be good." These thoughts are automatic. I always notice food or potential food. And Daantje keeps pieces and crusts of bread in his pockets and in his bed.

In the hot hours of late afternoon we interrupt our play to buy ice cream from the vendor, who tinkles his bell to announce his coming down the block. One afternoon I meet two brothers, cousins also, who live with their mother in an apartment not far away. Their father was caught by the Gestapo in Holland, while they got out of Europe just in time. I really like every one of the relatives I've met here. I think that Rena and Ellen, Aunt and Uncle, and Great Aunt Lily are very good to me. I'm not sure what I mean but there is such a safe feeling being with these relatives. I love hearing Aunt and Uncle talk and joke with each other. The girls quarrel and sometimes try to cajole their father to buy them something. It's intriguing to watch them be children in their family. I look on from a far distance. One afternoon I overhear Mama in conversation with Aunt and Great Aunt. Mama's voice is angry and sarcastic, accusing them of something I don't understand. A miserable mix of feelings rushes through me. I feel so sorry for Mama but also deeply shamed by her outburst and terribly uneasy.

Friday evening Aunt and Uncle light the Shabbat candles and say the blessings. It's very different from when I was little but I'm glad every Friday evening. It's different because here in this family they don't "keep Shabbat." We don't go to services. I don't dress festively. Saturday is no longer a day set apart. Aside from Friday evening the day is like any other day of the week.

One very hot day Uncle and Aunt take us all to the ocean. After a long car ride we come to the widest beach I've ever seen. They settle by a little hut called a cabana. Unlike the North Sea where dunes range the long distances to keep the ocean waves from the land, these beaches, immense and flat, allow for long curling waves that finally eddy out in small swooshes, recurling endlessly. In the roaring, reaching waves I discover a wonderful game. I let myself go limp and lie in the water to be rolled around and heaved close and closer to the shore. At the sandy edge the last motions continue to gently roll me, seep under, around and over me. As if I'm water, as if I'm sand, I lose the me and find . . . everything. The sky, the sun heat, the water wet, the enveloping roar, I'm not in me; I'm in all of it. The feeling is not in words. I feel it again and again as I let my body go utterly free again and again in the water roar, rolling waves. Is what I am doing playing? The feeling that has no words is happy, happy.

How long are we in New York? Four weeks? Five, six? Surely not more than eight weeks. One afternoon Rena and I shower together to cool off and clean up before supper. Looking at Rena's body makes me look at my own body. She is all smooth as if made of softly stretched velvet. But I, I am made of bones, knobs, corners. Nowhere on my body do I see her smoothness. I am startled by my own ugliness. I didn't know before that I looked like this. I never noticed!

Mama took Daantje away to visit the other relatives on the farm. After our first weeks in New York he went to hospital to have his tonsils removed. Then he was here in bed, sick for a while. Mama says that during the vacation months of summer he will be sent to summer camp and I will go to the farm. The farm is in New York state but so far away that you have to ride on the train for hours, maybe most of the day.

Mama is going to Chicago to live with Tante Lisel. In September Daantje and I will go to Chicago to join them. Why does Mama go to Chicago? I want to stay here. Tante Lisel came to New York to meet us. I'm supposed to like her but I didn't much. I love Uncle Hans and Aunt Olga. I like having cousins. I'm happy to stay here. Strangely Daantje's disappearances don't worry me anymore.

Being with the relatives is like sinking into a warm feather comforter. It is being fed and being cared for. But more than that it is no longer having to worry about Mama. It is as if a room that is darkened by shade-covered windows now suddenly brightens and shows its interior textures and colors. Being with the relatives is like being in heaven. I feel love toward them. And they like me. I know it, I feel it, and that is like being in heaven.

I have no sense of saying good-bye to Uncle and Aunt, or Rena and Ellen, or the boy cousins. I have no sense that I will ever see them again after Mama and I leave. Thrown into this utterly new life for these brief weeks, I'm suddenly whisked away again.

The train to the farm carries Mama and me through beautiful country. There are hills, mountains practically, and rivers. I talk to Mama about school in the fall. I say that all I need is a skirt and two scotch plaid blouses. I can see myself looking nice wearing that. I know Mama is worried about earning money. So that's how I reassure her that I won't need much. But it's also my way of telling her it's important to me that I can have two scotch plaid blouses. It gives me a picture of myself that I like. Mama nods her head but doesn't say anything. I don't know this yet, but I am trying very, very hard to hold onto a picture of myself.

17

THE FARM

The farm is a house on a hill, and at the bottom of the hill across the road a barn and another smaller barn. In between the barns, a slow-moving creek, a pond made by Uncle Walter, and a huge, wonderful oak tree straddling the creek bed. The pond holds ducks. Up behind the white painted house is Aunt Rena's garden, growing herbs and vegetables. A grassy lawn slopes in front of the house and there is a round flower bed and some big trees to give shade. Alongside the house is a track where a car can be parked. The track runs down the hill alongside a red painted shed to the road. In the shed stands Uncle Walter's car. On the high, dry side of the big barn the huge hanging doors are open and there stands a wagon and toward the side edging the field is some machinery whose names I don't know. Inside the barn are cows, two big horses, and countless cats and kittens.

In the house live Aunt Rena, Uncle Walter, and their little girl, Becky. Great Aunt Lily is there also. She has a room of her own, off the living room. Her room is full of dark furniture and books. Up the stairs, one room is for Uncle and Aunt. One room is for Jake, and one is for Don. Jake and Don help Uncle with the summer farm work. During the year they study at a university. The fourth room is for Becky, and I have a bed there, too. The best room is the big kitchen, with a big table snuck into one corner by the big window.

Very soon Uncle Peter and his wife come to visit. They are traveling all the way to California. Uncle Peter is a teacher and his wife writes stories. I like him. He plays catch with me and talks with me. I am learning to understand English. Although I think in Dutch I am beginning to talk

132

English, too. They give me a wonderful present: a book called *On to Oregon*. I begin reading and I can understand it! I have to ask them to explain a few words but I can really follow the story. A pioneer farming family with many children travels the Oregon Trail to settle on new land. The mother and father die on the way. Then the oldest boy who is thirteen and the next oldest brother and sister travel on, taking care of the younger kids and a new baby who almost dies. After many scary adventures and terrible hardships they do arrive in Oregon and settle with a wonderful doctor-missionary and his wife. The book says the story is real; there are historical records of their going to the Willamette Valley. I understand the oldest boy the best, because he is rebellious and thinks the grownups are fools for the most part. And he's scared a lot of the time but he makes himself and the other kids keep on traveling. Their hunger and cold are familiar but this is a story and none of the kids dies. Nobody hates them and the family they come to are ready to love them.

This story book is the beginning of my learning about America. It also is the beginning of playing long, solitary games of pioneer and Indian. Everything in the story becomes part of my imagination. In Uncle's barnyard, I climb the huge oak tree and the branch I sit on is my horse. I look through the green leaves and pretend I'm escaping from Indians or riding unseen through the land.

Of course I don't play like this all the time because there are many things to do on the farm. Becky is five and she and I can go with Uncle to ride on top of wagons piled with alfalfa or peas. We go with Aunt to pick blackberries in the thick, thorny bushes that edge the fields. Before supper I can go to the kitchen garden to cut fresh dill for the cottage cheese. I can pull weeds to give the good vegetables room to grow. Aunt sends me to collect the eggs in the small barn. Not even to myself do I want to admit how scared I am of the chickens. I think they will fly up to peck at my face and eyes. I set my teeth, screw my eyes together, and quick as I can feel for the eggs. Done! Until tomorrow.

At milking time we go to the barn to play, sometimes to let the new, smallest calves suck on our fingers. How strong they suck! The mooing, moving, chewing cows and the men busy with the milking pails, giving cows a shove or pat, talking their men's talk, indefinably different than the talk up at the house—the smelly, warm livingness of the cows are lovely. Lovely, alive. I'm alive. In the barn the prickling hay, the leather harnesses, the bins of feed, the nails and bits of tool parts, my own body in a red and white playsuit with white sneakers, sweating, breathing the smells, the heated air, the whiff of breeze. My own arms and legs, alive, oh, God, running, rolling in the deep grass down the slope from the house, alive! The farm is heaven. Can I stay here? It would be wonderful to stay here!

The nearest neighbors live in a tiny house on a hilltop with a yard full of old car parts, tractor pieces, a small kitchen garden, and a square of clothesline. There are four girls and a baby brother. The oldest girl is even older than I am; the others fit between Becky and me. Their parents fight, and sometimes their father goes away for a while. Once I was up at their place and everyone was at the table to eat and I could feel the scared, tense feeling until the father seemed to explode and yell at the youngest girl. They are poor but come over lots and we play, especially after supper in the long hours before dark. Down the road farther is another house, unpainted, on a hill and the people who live there change all the time. Right now the family that lives there has two boys. I see them out in their yard sometimes when I ride by on Uncle's tractor. Those boys aren't allowed to leave their yard to come play, and once I looked up and saw them shirtless with belt marks on their backs. I feel bad for them and disgusted with the grownups they live with until one evening they come down to the meadow where we gather to play. They stand on the side and the older boy starts taunting me about how weird I talk. I'm a "dirty forriner!" He yells something else. I don't understand it because suddenly I'm flooded with rage. I think, "Yell, go ahead, yell, I'm glad your father beats you! I hope he beats you up again!" But afterward I realize with wonder that all the kids and grownups I've met so far are very nice to me and no one teases me because of my accent or lack of English. These boys are an absolute exception. Being on the farm is being in heaven. How can I begin to say for myself all the good things about being there?

One afternoon I get to ride on one of the big horses as they are led back to the barnyard. They lumber through the ridged, dried mud ruts under the big tree. Before I can yell, one of the branches has swept me off the horse and I've fallen backward, thudding to the ground. I'm knocked breathless but conscious. I see Uncle's frightened face as he peers down at me. I want to reassure him I'm all right, nothing broken, I'm not dead. It takes a minute before I can speak the words. It's just the same as when I was little and got knocked down in the schoolyard on my sixth birthday.

Everyone works hard. Uncle and the two young men who help him, Aunt, and Great Aunt Lily even. All are busy except after lunch when everyone sleeps for an hour or so. Because everyone works hard we have four meals a day: breakfast, dinner, tea, and supper. Uncle and the helpers get up long before I do to milk the cows. They come in stamping their feet, making comments about this cow or that one as they sit around the breakfast table. The radio voice gives farm news and weather reports and stories from little towns in the area. The English voice is a background noise and I understand less than half of it. Today is special because after the morning's work and the after-dinner nap we are going on a picnic.

In Uncle's car we drive to the little crossroads town nearest to the farm. There, in a big field, I see tables set up and a big tent and lots of people. Many ladies say hello to Aunt and Becky pulls me along to play with kids she knows. We can get lemonade to drink and there is a whole table with food and pies. It's sort of a happy confusion but what makes it so nice is the friendliness of the grownups. Everyone seems to know each other. Even if I don't know the kids it doesn't matter in the running around and in the games. Toward dusk there is a running race for all the kids. Me, too. I run as hard as I can and I win! Really! It doesn't seem possible I can win but the proof is the prize I can take to the lemonade or ice cream stand. I know I tried as hard as I could but I never thought I would be able to run the fastest! In Uncle's car on the way home Becky and I fall asleep. It is the Fourth of July, an American holiday.

Soon I learn that I have to leave for Chicago, a city far, far away. There I will live with Mama, Daantje, and Tante Lisel. There I will go to school. I haven't missed Mama at all and I don't want to leave here to go live with her. I don't tell anyone what I feel. I don't ask to stay. I don't even think about asking. Aunt Rena will take me to the train station and put me on the train. On a piece of paper I have the name of the train station and the address in Chicago where I am going.

I wave good-bye to Aunt Rena and wish she would hug me and not let me go away. I can imagine myself being part of her family. But as I wave through the train window, I see her turning away. In my mind I see her quickly stepping to the car. She will drive back to the farm and be busy immediately with supper preparation. Already I am not part of their life and already I miss the farm.

18

CHICAGO

The train hurtles fast. I look out until the light fades. I eat the sandwiches Aunt Rena packed for me. I fall asleep. A long time after it is light again, the conductor announces we'll be coming into Chicago. Now suddenly I'm terribly afraid. Where am I going? My paper slip says Englewood and Eggleston. They sound so alike. One is the name of the station and one is the name of the street. But which is which? I ask, I show the piece of paper to the conductor and other people on the train. They nod. They say, "We'll tell you where you have to get off." The train stops, I get off on a large, long platform, look around, and after a long minute see Mama, Daantje, and Tante Lisel in the distance. I feel . . . not happy, but oh, so relieved.

As we leave the train platform, I see that the street is lined with trees. Hungrily my eyes center on the green trees, familiar and beloved. We walk a few blocks and come to one of many little houses. I sense that Mama and Tante very much want me to like this house. It is nice, a house a child could draw with a triangle roof, a door, two front windows. What is completely strange is the porch in front and the bench hung from the ceiling by two chains so you can sit and gently swing. Inside, a living room to the right, a dining room directly ahead, and walking further back a kitchen with two windows overlooking a yard in back. The back door opens onto another porch. To the side of the kitchen is a bathroom. In American houses the toilet is inside the bathroom, not in a separate little cubicle, which is strange. Off the kitchen another door opens to a "pantry." Shelves of cans, spaces for noodles, potatoes, and sugar. Shelves of space for food! From the entry door, slightly left is a staircase

136

leading to the attic floor with sloping ceilings. There are two little rooms overlooking the back and one larger room overlooking the street. Behind the little garden in back is the "alley" and over the alley is a metal structure that carries the tracks for the "el." Soon I hear the noise of the approaching elevated train and for a moment the noise overtakes our speaking, hearing, our very breathing. Then it rumbles off into the distance.

One little room is for Daantje and one is for me. I've never had my own room; it even has a closet. There is a mirror on the wall and a desk and chair. A bed is pushed into one corner and the window, a dormer, looks onto the back porch roof. The bigger room in front is to be rented out so that Tante Lisel, who has bought this house, can get some money to help pay for it. Apparently, Mama and Tante looked for an apartment for us but no space was available and where there was space, children were not wanted. Tante is sorry that we cannot live in her neighborhood, Hyde Park. All her friends are there. Tante is a pharmacist who came to Chicago in the 1930s. The little house is in a neighborhood called Englewood.

The second evening, the doorbell rings. A lady stands by the door and announces that she wants to welcome us to the neighborhood. Does Mama know where to register us for school? The lady tells us that if there is anything we need we should call on her. She will help. She lives in a house on the next block and she is the "Democratic Committee woman." I've never met a grownup stranger so friendly. She talks about her daughter and tells us she is Irish. Somehow this seems important.

The following day, Mama, Daantje, and I walk about four blocks to the local public school, the Lewis Champlain School. There is no headmaster; there is a lady principal. Mama talks with her and says I was in sixth grade for a month in New York. The principal takes me to a seventh-grade class where the teacher is another lady. Like the principal she is Irish. It is now September 1947 and at the end of this month I will be twelve years old.

After the first few days, I see that the children are kind; no one appears to be mean. At recess I begin to make friends. The girls play a jumprope game called double dutch. I never saw this game in Holland. But the game is fun, fast, and almost everyone plays. During the play time I see the boys and girls, lively and interesting, although very foreign to me. But in the class time all has a deadened, dull feeling and the children seem bland. The building itself is unpleasant; there is no garden, the walls of the hall and classroom are painted a putrid green, and worst of all there is nothing interesting in the classroom. There are few books, no plants, no fish, no musical instruments, and there is no place to make things. It feels so barren.

In my class I become special friends with a girl who is taller than I am and smart and interesting. Delia has nine younger brothers and sisters! Her two older brothers are away in the army. Over time she points out all her other sisters and brothers. We understand each other and I really like her. Once Mama and I meet Delia's mother on the street wheeling the buggy with the twelfth baby. Mama says that it is remarkable how white and healthy Delia's mother's teeth are. Why? Because a woman often loses her teeth after so many babies, Mama explains to me.

Delia is mostly busy looking after kids at home; there isn't much time to play. I walk her home so that we can talk and we make the most of the time before and during school. When I go home with her for lunch one time, I understand immediately that her family is really poor. Although they live in a real house, lunch is a thin soup and salty soda crackers. I recognize that the little kids are still hungry but there isn't any more. I say I've had enough although I'm still rumbling with hunger. Delia's father is a taxi driver and there is never enough. Her parents are from far away; they come from the south and at school somebody says they are hillbillies, whatever that is. Delia seems like the smartest person in the class aside from two boys who also seem to know things and have sense. I wonder if they are as unhappy in this school as I am. But what I have to learn is English. I learn all the time, mostly from the kids.

This school, as miserable as it is, has one treasure. This treasure is the library. A classroom especially for this purpose has shelves all around it and some tables with chairs. A teacher is in charge and the room is open every day. We have a "period" when the whole class troops to the library. After the joy of reading *On to Oregon* I wonder if there are other marvelous stories to be found. The librarian teacher is a person I can respect. She talks to the kids as if they have some sense and she is quickly friendly to me and suggests books for me to read. When she sees me use my finger to follow where I am reading she tells me to try to do without that crutch. This advice I do not listen to; I know when something helps me or not, after all. Sometimes now I get permission to go to the library during a regular class, after I've finished the assignment. The Irish lady who is the teacher of my class seems a nice person although she doesn't have authority or knowledge in the way my teacher in Holland had. She tells us about the Depression when she knew people who were so poor and hungry that they searched the garbage cans for food. Mama has told me about the terrible depression in Germany after World War I, when she was a little girl, but I didn't know anything like that happened in America. Somehow I trust the teacher a little bit more after she tells us the Depression stories.

In the class the lessons are pages in a workbook and I can do the work almost by the time I see it on the page. A big part of the lessons is spelling. In my mind I say the words in Dutch, phonetically. That way it's easy to remember all the letters of an English word, even the ones that aren't spoken and the ones that seem to be there for no reason. In arithmetic, some of what the teacher shows us I already learned in Holland and the new ideas I learn quickly. The whole class has to work together so that if I finish after ten minutes, I still have to wait until the time for arithmetic is over. After a few weeks I begin to read a book while I wait. The atmosphere in the school is so foreign I can't make any sense of it. One of the first differences I notice is that here people can come into the class to interrupt the teacher and the lessons. I think it's rude to interrupt but also don't they think the lesson time is important? Something else that seems unpleasantly strange is how the teachers and the principal lady talk to the children. They pick on some boy or girl in a nasty way, but at the same time they aren't strict about the work and the kids don't respect the teachers. The kids are afraid, though, of getting into trouble. I don't understand that either because from what I can see no one gets hurt around here. Finally I figure that some of the kids would get into bad trouble at home if the teacher tells their parents and that's why they are scared. All of it feels inexpressibly strange and unpleasant. Was my school in Amsterdam that special? Is this what American schools are like?

However, I put to use my new knowledge that the kids here are afraid of the teachers. Something is happening at recess. As we play double dutch, there is a crucial moment when you have to jump into the moving double ropes. A girl from another class slaps my tush at the crucial moment and I miss the entry into the quick, clicking ropes. At first, astonished, I tell her not to do that. The next day and the day following she does it again. I begin to chase her so that I can make her stop. What's with this crazy kid? I've never even talked to her. For two weeks I chase her and learn that no matter how hard I try, I can't run fast enough to catch her. She doesn't stop bothering me so I have to find a way to stop her.

At the end of our play area is a parking area for the cars of the teachers. Beyond the parking area is the street. I've learned that it is the sin beyond sins to leave the play area or the school area. If I keep chasing her she'll be afraid to cross the street. So then she'll have to stop and face me. At the next recess she hits me again and I go after her. Sure enough, I chase her to the cars without catching her. Finally, in the middle of the parked cars she stops, turns, and I am at her with the rage of weeks of stored up frustration. She's bigger but I punch her a bloody nose. Along the way she knocks out my last remaining baby tooth that has been hanging by a thread for days. I keep punching wild with rage. The monitors come to pull us apart and walk us to the principal's office. Of course we are not supposed to fight. I don't care; I only regret I couldn't get her down on the ground, but she's too big for me. The principal lady says words to the girl and then she turns to me and asks if I'm hurt. No! I'm not hurt! But I'm crying with rage, incoherent in English or Dutch. Newly enraged to hear the principal lady think I could be hurt. When I calm down I begin to feel the fierce joy of knowing my plan worked! She'd better not bother me again, ever! And she doesn't, ever.

I read more and more. I lose myself in stories. I read when the lesson is boring, I read when I've finished my work, I read before I go to sleep. Sometimes I read a book in one day. I read about immigrants, about settling the wilderness, about Indians. I read about brave, happy families and stories set in Norway, Sweden, Hungary, and Holland, in ancient Egypt and the Revolutionary War. I read about children, abandoned, enslaved, or orphaned. Stories about adventure on the sea or on the land transport me. I learn American history, American geography, and American ideas from the books. A rich interior world is mine for the taking. To lose myself in the stories is wonderful because I'm in the imaginary world completely. I can shut out what is around me so that I don't hear and don't see. I can shut out what is inside me so that I don't have to feel or think.

Slowly, in the little house on Eggleston, a new routine of life unfolds for us. Mama goes to work everyday. She comes back in the evening and we have supper together. Tante works five and a half days a week. Three times a week she goes in the afternoon and comes home late at night when we are already in bed. On those days Tante makes supper ahead of time. All Mama has to do is finish everything because Mama doesn't know how to cook. At lunchtime Daantje and I come home together for a while but as the months go by we don't always go together anymore. He is making friends with a boy down the block. He plays in the alley with a bunch of boys. In the late afternoon we wait for Mama to come home. I am surprised at how alone I feel and how much I long for Mama to come home. On the days Tante works regular hours, we four together have supper sitting in the kitchen where the table is squarely in the middle of the room. Each night Daantje and I clean up.

Mama goes to lie down on her bed, the couch in the living room. She is very tired. Daantje and I create a cleaning-up routine which is something in between work and play. I wash the dishes, he dries. He cleans the table with the dishrag and throws it back to me, aiming at my head, which he always misses. I sing every song I know while we clean up and usually we are laughing about something when Mama's voice sounds, "Please children can you be a little quiet? I have such a headache." We try but our version of quiet is not Mama's version of quiet.

The first months the three of us still have our once-a-week special tea time with cookies and games. It still feels special but is experienced alongside all the new strange ways and language we are learning. That seems to take the edge off that special feeling. Or maybe it feels different because I am growing up and I am different.

My first growing-up sign came to me the morning of my twelfth birthday. I awoke and went downstairs to pee. As I wiped myself, I see the toilet paper red. More paper fills with thick red blood. I sit, stunned. And then I think, "Oh no, not yet, not already, I am not ready, I need more time. . . ." At school the following days I'm afraid to move. I can feel the warm flow and I'm sure that if I stand up every one will see because my skirt will be stained with blood. For some months there are moments of agonizing embarrassment but slowly periods become a familiar, if bothersome, happening. Mostly periods just make me very tired. Sometimes I get cramps in my belly that hurt enough so that they can't be ignored. Once in a while, they get bad and I, trying to take a nap, am writhing on the bed instead.

After some months, Daantje and I answer in English when Mama talks to us in Dutch. Daantje even gets a new nickname: Dannio. Did the boys give him that nickname? I don't know but I do know I have to call him by an affection name, never just Daan. I read and reread the Dutch books I brought with me although I am unaware that a person can lose the speaking ability in a language if she doesn't hear it for a long time. Mama learns to speak English, too. She learns at the corset shop where she works, sewing. She studied English long, long ago in school when she still lived in Frankfurt. Soon her use of Dutch fades as she becomes more fluent in English. Dutch was a second language for her and actually how many years did she really have to learn to speak it? Four or five years at the most.

In the winter my class holds a spelling bee and I get as far as one out of the last two children. I'm eliminated but secretly I think that it's strange I can win over the other children in the class who know English. At mid-year I am put in an "eight B" class, skipping the second half of the seventh altogether.

The teacher for this class is an exact opposite of the first teacher lady. Where she was sweet, this one is sarcastic. Where she was quiet and seemed kind, this one is angry and seems bitter. I sit in this class hating how she looks, hating the sound of her voice, and despairing because I am not learning anything! I am afraid I'll forget everything I learned in my school in Holland. There are just a few brown children in the class. This teacher, who is a hateful, mean person, seems especially sarcastic to the brown children. Everyone seems to react to her the same way. She attacks and humiliates someone and then they are hardly able to answer any questions she asks. The brown children get even more quiet than the others.

One late winter afternoon I walk by the school and look up to the windows of my classroom. I have an impulse to throw a rock through these windows; that's how much I hate this miserable place, that's how much I hate being here. I stop to talk with one of the girls I know. As we stand in the Chicago wind, she word-fights with a couple of brown girls. She calls them names and has an ugly, hateful tone in her voice. The brown kids shout back. The sounds blow away from us as I stand at the apex of a triangle, looking at the brown kids, then at the white girl. The hate-filled abuse voice is so familiar; I did not know I would hear it again, here in America. I look and want the girl to stop, "It's not right, don't do that!" I want to walk over to the brown kids to show solidarity but I don't move and I don't say a word. I'm caught already in the net; knowing I'd be ostracized if I take the brown kids' part. I can't decide quickly enough to act on my own belief and take the risk.

Over the past months I've been learning the spoken and unspoken attitudes of the people here to the brown people they call Negroes. It's true that the first time I saw a Negro person in New York I stared. That's because during the first days I couldn't believe people can look so incredibly different from me. But after some months in Chicago, the brown kids don't look that different. They are just foreign like all the others at school. But as we meet neighbors and Mama becomes friends with a lady down the block, and I start meeting the mothers of my new friends, a very strange realization comes to me. Most of these people are welcoming and very pleasant. They seem like good people except when someone mentions Negroes. Then I hear angry, nasty things said. What makes people so angry? Not everyone is like that. It's a huge relief when I'm with someone who doesn't have that attitude. But causing even more puzzlement and discomfort is the realization that people absolutely want you to agree, to think the same way. Somehow, the message is clear; think like we do or be a despicable outsider. So far, I can't make any sense of it. But these hate-filled attitudes make me frightened inside. I know, I know people like that can't be trusted.

I think that all the people who said or thought bad things about Jews . . . they didn't take us to Bergen-Belsen themselves. They didn't guard us themselves but they made it possible for other people to do it. Don't they understand? Don't they understand they are responsible? I feel the people who talk bad about Negroes are the same. They themselves don't do anything evil to another person but they make it possible for some people to do really evil things to Negro people. I think that.

In New York one of the relatives took Mama and me to a big store. There they bought me underwear, a skirt, two pretty blouses, a dress, socks, and shoes. From a friend we get a package of used playclothes and "jeans." I get to wear white tennis shoes, my favorite thing! But better than all these is a little gold Star of David on a gold chain. Great Aunt Lily had given it to me. Mama doesn't want me to wear it so I hide it under my clothes. In the little attic room I treasure some other possessions: the Boy Scout belt that I talked Daantje into giving me, and some transparent scarves with lovely patterns that I collected in Holland. In the small mirror hanging on my wall I see myself veiled by one of these scarves. I play. I play by myself in the little attic room. Here I am not Dutch, not American, not Jewish, not . . . I am a guerilla fighter! I am a girl fighter who is the leader, helping my imaginary group plan an ambush or fighting in order to retreat safely to a hiding place. Sometimes I am a girl guerilla who dances for her group with the veils, intriguing my group, who think I'm beautiful.

Tante Lisel has introduced us to her hiking club. Every Sunday we take the streetcar or train a long way to meet a small group of other people. We follow a leader to find a park or country area to walk in. It's a joy to get out of the city, and Daantje and I are content to join the adults. There are no other children and some of the adults are immigrants, too. In cold winter weather we hike, too, bundled up to be comfortable. One of the hiking friends is a nice man who talks to Tante and Mama. To my surprise he comes to the little house one Saturday. He is taking me to a shop to buy a Schwinn bike! We walk a long way and pick out a girl's

143

bike by color. I like blue. He says I should try riding it to see if that is what I really want. What I want? I am quietly humming with pleasure. This, this is a fabulous present. A real birthday present from the relatives in New York. After this shopping expedition I imagine that if Tony would marry Mama, I would feel happy. Not that I think in any way he would be like Papa, but somehow everything would be more right. Maybe that horrible hollowed-out aching that I feel in my chest all the time would go away, maybe a little bit of it would go away.

Tante likes to cook. Tante has friends. One family of friends joins us for a festive evening. Two boys and one girl who have been in the States longer than we and to me seem already American. They are refugees, too, but have come from some South American country. The father grew up in Berlin and seems hopelessly "German," bossy. About him I never dream wish fantasies that he could marry Mama and become our papa.

Tante likes to read. She likes poetry. She also likes Daantje. She and he joke around and find things to laugh about. But the laughing doesn't include me; it doesn't touch me. I don't think Tante likes me much. Most mornings she complains that I didn't clean the kitchen well enough. The coal furnace in the basement has to be checked after school. Sometimes it is out when I come home and then I have to relight it. I can't always get the fire going again although Daantje seems to know how to refire the coals. I begin to believe that Tante doesn't think much of me and that I don't ever do things right or do enough in her opinion.

One evening, during supper, Tante and Mama start arguing. We sit at the square kitchen table, Mama and Tante across from each other and Daantje and I across from each other, listening. The argument goes on and on. After we finish eating, they still are fighting. I go upstairs to my little room but the fighting voices pursue me. The next morning is a Sunday, everyone is home. I find Mama and ask her when we are leaving. She looks at me without expression, without understanding. I ask, "Aren't we leaving after you fought so last night?" I can't imagine staying together after such a fight, but Mama says, "Ach, of course not, it's nothing." I'm not reassured. In the days that follow there is a predictable pattern. When Tante and Mama are home together, sooner or later there is a quarrel. There are no screams, no doors slamming, no one stomping out of the house. No, what there is, is an unrelenting low rumbling quarreling about . . . about what? I can't understand what they fight about. They just disagree about everything. I think if one says the sky is blue, the other would say the sky is green. The worst is that no one else seems to mind especially. For me the constant quarreling is as if mosquitoes have been set loose to zing inside my skull. There is peace when Mama, Daantje, and I are home alone. I begin to feel that our times alone, just us, in Amsterdam and here, are priceless. I almost forget how miserable I sometimes feel around Mama. One morning I say to Tante, "You shouldn't talk to Mama like that!" Tante looks at me and almost smiles, "You don't have to defend your mother now." Yes, I do. I do have to defend her. On the evenings Tante works late at the pharmacy, I lie awake to hear her come home. I hear the raised voices and lie in bed, utterly miserable, unable to quiet my mind.

Before I sleep I talk to God. Every night I say the same thing, "Please, dear God, give me strength, make me strong, please dear God give me strength." Why do I pray? Why do I talk to God when I think there cannot be God? I pray because I have to talk to someone. I am so alone and I'm afraid. I'm afraid of my dreams at night. I never know if I'll have a terrible nightmare. When I have bad dreams, I wake up in the morning feeling so awful that it takes all my strength to get up, face the family downstairs, and get going for school. One night I bump myself awake as I've fallen out of bed; sometimes I wake in the morning on the floor without ever knowing how I got there.

I know I have a "double-track" life now. On the outside, what Mama and other people see is a girl who is learning English fast, who has two new friends on the block, who has friends at school, who is doing so well at school that she is promoted to the eighth grade. They see a girl who laughs and plays, giggles with her friends, reads, and rides her bike. Inside me is fear. My dreams scare me. When I'm awake I'm afraid of my memory. Whole days in Bergen-Belsen flash through on my brain's inner screen. But most of all I fear a "breaking inside" feeling. I try not to feel it. I try my hardest to control it. I tell myself not to be "sentimental." Somehow the American kids are not emotional; when I'm with them I feel freaky, as though something is wrong with me feeling so much, feeling so strongly. So I begin to call every feeling "sentimental" and to be sentimental is bad.

Mama has urged me to go to the local YMCA because they have a swimming pool and I could go swimming again. At first I object; I hear the word "Christian" in the YMCA name and feel only fear and unease and despair. But after some days I do go and soon I'm enrolled in a gym and swim program. I go there twice a week. Far from being dangerous to me, the YMCA program begins to feel like a twice-a-week rescue. I become part of a small group of girls ranging in age from twelve to fifteen who are the best swimmers. The swim/gym coach treats us as group and begins to do special activities with us. We compete in swim meets and diving events, we do water ballet to put on shows for parents and other adults, we help teach the little kids swimming during school vacations, we meet as a "girls club" and we go camping. Soon I decide that our counselor, Betty, is just everything I'd like to be. She is skilled in baseball, volleyball, and basketball, and she is a real American grownup. She's my heroine. Now, the only person who matters to me is Betty and the only times in the week when I feel happy are the swim times at the "Y." The girls tease me but it's in a fun, friendly way. While I'm with them I feel a part of this little group. They ask me to say "crazy" and laugh at my pronunciation; soon my nickname is "crazy."

Another nickname I get is "giggles" because it often happens now that I start laughing and then it goes out of control. The giggling starts to feel bad. Although I try and try I cannot control what happens as my body shakes and trembles with the gusts of giggling. Even so, having a nickname feels special.

At home, I wash the dishes and on Saturday, I'm supposed to wash our laundry. In the basement are two tubs. One soaks the sheets, towels, underwear, and shirts. In the other I scrub each piece on a scrubbing board and then wring dry the various pieces. They are hung over clotheslines strung across the basement. Mama helps me wring the sheets. Usually I play in the soapy water and draw pictures on the soap before I get to work. Soon one of my "Y" friends comes by on a bike and asks, "Aren't you done? Can you come out to play?" That helps me hurry to finish the washing. I also take the weekly grocery list to the store and cart the bags home in a little rolling cart. The store is only a block away.

A year later we buy a washing machine and now Mama or Tante do the laundry. There is a mangler through which each piece goes to press out all the water. It isn't safe for a kid to use and sure enough even Mama gets her hand caught in the mangler and has to wear a bandage for many days. Now I do the ironing for the family. This is more fun than the laundry. I iron on Saturday afternoon when the Metropolitan Opera Company has its weekly broadcast. We've just recently bought a radio and I begin to listen to music and fall in love. In love with opera and symphonic music I hear once or twice a week. I listen to Beethoven and decide that this is the most perfect music there is. I think that it was worth living through everything just to be able to hear this music!

The radio offers up another treasure: spoken English. I listen to hear how it should sound. It's different from how the kids talk. Once when Oma's sister, Tante Lily, came to visit us from New York, she took me for a walk. She said, "You must say 'is not' instead of 'ain't' and say 'doesn't' instead of 'don't'." She made other suggestions and said I must learn good English. I shouldn't listen to how the kids talk but teach myself to speak well. So the radio is very helpful even though there is a lot I don't understand. The hardest to understand are the comedy shows. I listen to the words, I know what they mean, but strung together they don't make sense to me. Then I hear the audience's rumbling laughter. It's so strange to hear this hearty guffawing and be left totally outside of it because it just doesn't mean anything to me. For my thirteenth birthday I get a little radio to have in my room. So now I can listen to mystery programs at night. English and more English, but these programs I can follow, even though the world of "Superman," "The Lone Ranger," "The Shadow," "Stella Dallas," and "One Man's Family" broadcast a world too weird to be believed. Fortunately you don't have to believe to be entertained.

The radio also brings news. Winston Churchill makes a speech about the Russians. They, who conquered half of Germany, also conquered the other countries in between themselves and Germany. Churchill says the Russians are doing bad things and that there is an "iron curtain hanging" between the western allies and the Russians. It's hard to hear bad things about the Russians, our liberators. On the other hand, Churchill has been a hero for a long time and so are the Americans and other English speakers. This is in spite of the fact that it is the English who won't let us go to Palestine. But other news reports bring the unbelievable event of the English pulling out of Palestine and the declaration of Israel's national existence. Mama and Tante don't talk much about the news. There is no one else around to talk with so I try to think this through myself in the little room upstairs. More than ever I wish I could go to Israel. There no one could tell me not to celebrate Shabbat or the holidays. No one there would tell me that I can no longer be a Jewish girl.

I know that slowly I'm forgetting what some of the Jewish holidays are. It's been such a long, long time since we lived altogether in Amsterdam. America is so far away, so far away from Israel that I cannot find a way to imagine how I could get myself there. A part of me also knows that I could never leave Daantje and Mama. But I feel that Israel is the place where I should be, where I really belong, where I might not be so afraid, where I might feel at home, happy even. I cannot forgive my own inability and cowardice in not figuring out a way to get there.

In some ways I can understand Mama's wish that we no longer be Jews. She wants to keep us safe. But I do not understand how Mama can live without Jewish neighbors or friends, without celebration. My new friends from the block, from school, from the "Y" are either Catholic or Protestant. Their parents, when I meet them are usually pleasant, sometimes very nice. But I always feel a huge hole . . . something important is missing. Once I ask Mama, "Doesn't it bother you? People are very nice but it seems so barren, so flat." Mama looks and shrugs. She has no answer. Maybe it doesn't bother her in the same way. I don't yet understand that what I try to express to her is my experiencing terrible loss. She doesn't understand because she doesn't feel it the same way I feel it. But I don't understand that Mama has her own categories of experience rooted in the upper middle-class life of a German Jewish family. She lost her papa when she was five years old; her initial world was shattered by World War I, and her youth defined by the virulent atmosphere in Germany.

One of the first questions the American kids ask is, "What are you?" And what they mean is "What religion are you? Where do you go to church?" I completely misunderstand this question. I hear a demand and I hear danger. I freeze inside and hold myself very still. I try out several answers, trying to find an answer that will make them leave me alone, make them stop asking questions. I answer, "I'm American now" or "I'm nothing" or "I'm Jewish but don't observe anything." Not one of these answers satisfies. The answers don't satisfy me either. Because I can't say surely and proudly, "I'm Jewish," in the act of answering I'm made aware of how scared and discomfited I feel. I don't want to feel so scared. I don't even want to know that I feel scared. But there is no escape.

Various friends from the "Y" want me to come visit their church with them. For many weeks I say no, no I don't want to. One of the girls asks me, "Don't you want to be saved?" I don't understand, what is she talking about? Saved from what? She's very serious: "You have to believe in Jesus Christ and then you'll be saved. Otherwise you go to hell when you die." Quietly I say, "I don't believe that." There is an insistence in her, a wish to convince me that sets my ears burning. If that's how Christians feel then they'll never leave us alone. I don't believe in a hell where bad people go after they die to suffer forever. What a terrible idea! Uneasily I realize that what I believe is that people themselves create hell while we live and that's exactly what the Germans and the people of other countries who helped them did.

Often now I feel shame. At home Mama or Tante Lisel scold because I haven't cleaned the kitchen well enough or because I let the furnace go out or because I didn't vacuum the downstairs and staircase. Mama

148

starts talking about how the girls in the family of neighbors do so much more to help. I listen and one part of me gets angry but another bigger part says, "Ok, ok, you're right, I should do more, willingly I should do more, I feel so bad already you don't have to keep saying it, stop it, stop it." I think this but don't say it aloud. When Daantje doesn't take the garbage out Mama screams at him and he temper-tantrums back at her. She starts hitting him with the broom and I'm afraid he'll start fighting back. The tension is unbearable and so to my immediate and everlasting shame I push him to the ground while Mama hits him. Until now I had always felt sorry for him when Mama got after him but in the last few months I'm aware of being irritable with him most of the time. It doesn't feel good but I seem to have no control over how quickly I get mad at him.

One evening Mama comes home tired and sick. I make supper though I hardly know what I'm doing. We sit down, he takes a spoonful of soup and says, "Yuch, this tastes like dishwater!" My rage is as much about the knowledge that I did the work, he didn't do a thing, as it is about the insult. I let loose the cup of hot cocoa in my hand and throw it at him, aware that I will miss his head. The cocoa splatters all over the wall. My rage is relieved and as I take a rag to wipe up the spill, I half laugh at myself.

A late winter afternoon Daantje and I get into a fight and he makes a discovery. He takes my long hair and pulls and suddenly my bigger size doesn't count as he pulls me into the front hall. At that moment the doorbell rings and through the glass door I see one of my friends. Half laughing, half mad, I open the door to explain what's going on. A part of me thinks, "Good for you, Daantje!" His discovery puts an end to our physical fights. The constant irritation with him that I felt so many months vanishes.

At the "Y" pool one afternoon I rub my neck and dirt comes off. I rub my neck some more and suddenly realize that all around my neck it's very dirty! I look around hoping no one will see me. My shamed feeling seems to spread from the bottom of my feet to the top of my head. Clearly our habit of once-a-week bath isn't good enough here. On an overnight camping trip, Betty asks, "Do you have some clean underwear?" I packed my stuff and never thought of extra underwear. Now I know I have to think carefully before I go on another trip. But these experiences are shaming from outside of me. On another weekend trip we have to walk into our camping place. After the truck drives us in, we unload our goods and figure out how to carry the bags and groceries, distributed among us. This time the thought, "I'll work hard so that they'll let me be with them and let me be alive," floods me. I am horrified and shamed that I think this. I try to push this idea out of my mind. But there is a small corner of me that knows I believe I've no right to be alive.

Not only my mind but my body, too, does unpredictable strange things. Shortly after coming to live in the little Eggleston Street house I notice that each time I get up from a chair I cannot see. My eyes register a thick, black filter on which grayish diagonals of dull light shimmer. As I slowly stand up this fleece before my eyes thins while the funny dizziness fades. Again I can see. One day standing in the grocery checkout line, I suddenly feel my bones soften and slackly fall to the ground while a small part of me knows I'm fainting. It gets worse. It happens more and more. During a swimming competition at the "Y" I swim the last length of my heat entirely unable to see because of the dark fleece before my eyes. I just keep going until I feel the edge of the pool. After Tante notices what is happening to me a visit to the doctor is arranged. A blood test gives a name for what is happening to me. I am very, very anemic. Every week I now have to go to the doctor's office to get an iron shot. I walk about twenty minutes south of where I live to his house in a pretty neighborhood. The front part is the office and there is a nurse who asks if I want to see my blood cells under the microscope. The shots aren't too bad but what is annoying is that the next day my thigh and tush ache. The achiness lasts for days. Then one or two days before the next shot is due it doesn't hurt anymore. The doctor is white-haired, gruff, and cheery. When he once remarks that I have the hide of an elephant I'm only half embarrassed. Mostly I'm a little insulted. I want to be pretty. Somehow having tough skin doesn't fit with my idea of "pretty." But over time the shots help and I don't black out anymore. But the shots don't take away the tiredness I feel all the time.

Dannio now has a very best friend from down the block. At school and after they spend all their time together. Dannio also starts reading about insects. He brings home book after book about the intriguing world of beehives, ant colonies, spiders and their webs. He loves all the science books he reads but especially the insect books. Mama has started to go to the high school for evening classes. She will learn to use office machines and more English so that she can get work in an office instead of sewing in the corset shop. I am going to start high school. At the eighth-grade graduation the teachers ask me to write a little speech. I did that and of course I wrote about some of the good things in coming to America. When Betty looked at my speech she said, "You didn't write this by yourself, did you?" I am surprised she asked me that. Of course I wrote it by myself; it's an honor to be asked to do this. When I gave the speech at graduation I'm not even too nervous.

Going to high school is a problem. The neighbors tell Mama that I shouldn't go to Englewood High School because all the children there are Negro children. The girls and boys from my class are going either to Catholic schools or to the technical high schools for boys or the secretarial high school for girls. About seven of us start at another school in the neighborhood but a little farther away called Parker High School. The first two days there seem very confusing. On the third day we are called to the office and told we cannot go to this school because it is "out of district." So on this day I am thrown out of school with the others. I and two or three others go to Englewood, register in the office, and get a class schedule. So far I think nothing of it. Since graduation was in winter, the high school semester will be from February to June. The next half year is the strangest, loneliest time yet since coming to America.

I'm small; most of the kids seem much bigger. It's hard to understand the English the kids speak. The classes are much larger than they were at the grade school. Each class has a teacher but nothing happens in the class. I'm signed up for algebra but the only thing the class covers is some simple math facts. I'm signed up for Latin but the only thing the class covers is the first three chapters of the Latin book in the whole half year! The most bizarre is the English class. I'm amazed to see the kids come into class with romance magazines and comic books. Everyone reads these while the teacher sits in the front. Is he asleep? Is he drunk? He has brown, nicotine-stained fingers for sure. The only thing he does is to pass out the long strips of paper the schools use for spelling tests. On the board he writes the same list of words every week. The test is to write the correct verb contractions—is not = isn't, do not = don't, etc. After the first week he walks to my desk and says, "Hurry up, aren't you finished yet?" When I finish he brings the papers to me to check and return to his desk. This is the English class, day after day after day.

Only the science teacher is active. The class is freshman biology. There is no lab or any material in the room. He mostly talks about what he requires of us. We are to make a "biology notebook." It's very hard for me to understand what I'm supposed to do. At least there is a cute girl who sits in front of me. She seems nice and we start to talk. After a few days I ask her if she wants to come over to my house for lunch. We walk the four blocks to my house, talking. We eat our sandwiches by the small square kitchen table. On the walk back I think that maybe I'll make a new friend. I look forward to the next day's biology class. I slide into my seat, lean over to say hi. She doesn't turn, doesn't say a word. I try again. No word, no look, as if I don't exist. About ten minutes into the class I understand. She isn't going to talk to me. She isn't going to be friends. The message is clear, "Don't make friends with a white kid." I look around, feel myself the immigrant stranger but with an added kick. I'm the only white kid in the class. In the halls passing from one class to another I'm aware of five or six other white kids from the neighborhood. The rest of the semester has a quality of mind-breaking aloneness, mind-numbing loneliness and boredom. Reading and the twice weekly swim sessions with my "Y" friends aren't enough to make up for the dragging days I sit through at this high school.

Tante Lisel has some friends who work at the University of Chicago. One day I'm told how to get to Hyde Park, find the Oriental Institute, and there ask to speak to Mr. G. Afterward I'm to stay overnight with Mr. G and his wife. I find the professor on the second floor in a small office overflowing with books. He asks me questions and chats with me about Tante Lisel and Mama. Later at his apartment, they are so sweet and attentive that it's like a dream. Mrs. G brings hot milky tea to drink, sits by my bed, and talks with me. I play chess with Mr. G. Weeks after this visit I'm called to the school office. An unknown lady has come to talk with me. I have no idea who she is or what she wants. We go into a small room and she asks me many questions. When she starts asking about Europe I feel myself getting angry and closed up. So then I answer only with a short "no" or "yes." Some time later Tante Lisel explains to me that I may be able to go to the private high school that is a part of the University of Chicago. It's known locally as the "Lab School." But first I have to go there on a Saturday morning to take a scholarship test. From my house to the streetcar to the Lab School takes almost an hour. In a room full of kids I take the exam and recognize many answers. When I learn that I've been admitted to the school and awarded a scholarship, I get an inkling of my good fortune. Finally I understand that Tante Lisel's friends made inquiries, that someone arranged for an application and a chance for me to take the entrance and scholarship test. I'll start the first year of high school again in September 1949 when I have my fourteenth birthday.

But beforehand, this summer I'll have my first part-time job like a real American girl. One of my older "Y" friends used to work for a lady with two little girls. She's recommended me because she, Kay, isn't free this summer. The lady works as a waitress. She doesn't have a husband

and the girls are six and four. I find the apartment on the second floor facing a busy street. The lady's work is in a restaurant on the corner of 63rd Street, three blocks from where she lives. She interviews me and tells me what I have to do. She hires me, I'm happy, and I don't even know enough yet to know to be scared of the responsibility. I have to be there at noon and she'll come home just after eight. The little girls play outside with a gang of other kids, or sit on the stoop drinking kool-aid. The six-year-old is easy and helpful. The four-year-old is harder to take care of. She's mischievous and doesn't always do what I tell her to do. I know how to give them supper because their mother always leaves hot dogs or peanut butter, jelly, and bread ready for them. I know how to help them wash their hands and face and get ready for bed. I know how to sing a song with them. What I don't know is what to do when something unusual happens.

One hot afternoon I look around for the littlest one and can't see her. I look up and down the block, ask her sister, ask the other kids. No one has seen her. Has she run away, did she get run over? Oh God, did she get kidnapped? Panicked, I ask some of the kids to help me look and I run around to the next street trying to find her, calling "Patricia!" over and over. If I've lost the lady's little girl it will be the most horrible thing in my life! Where is she? We look and look for what seems forever. Much later among another little group of playing kids I see her. She did go around the corner to another street. Her sister and I tell Patricia how she must never, ever, ever again go away like that. In the evening after the little girls are asleep, I finally absorb the relief and thankfulness that nothing bad happened to Patricia. But now I marvel at the poverty of this lady who has to have someone as young and unknowing as me take care of her little girls.

Often the lady comes home later because she couldn't leave work on time. I walk home in the dark and one night a man walks by me and says, "You want to f—— baby?" It's strange how you know what something means without knowing the words. I cross the street, walk fast, and feel very relieved when I get to 63rd Street, which is lit and has people out walking. The following year my friend Kay is accosted and, hanging onto her purse, fighting back her assailant, she is knifed to death on her parents' doorstep. I hear this news on the radio and when I go to the "Y" I casually tell the kids, "Kay is dead." They look at me strangely. Later Betty gets confirmation and details of what happened to Kay. I feel a fleeting sadness for Kay's parents. What could be worse than having your own child die? I join the others at the funeral. The church is big. Kay's high school friends are there, neighbors, family, so many people. Sobbing, speeches by friends, a long talk by the minister about the Kay he knew and about her family. I sit and all I feel is anger. "Why are they carrying on so much, it's just one girl who died . . . so . . . she's dead." Suddenly I think, "No one says words for my Papa, for Oma, for all my friends, for those forever many, many people who all died, forever and ever." I can't feel sad. I liked and admired Kay because she was a very hardworking, cute, spunky girl. I can't feel sad. I feel. . . . Harsh? Cynical? The kids still look at me. I understand. It's because I don't fuss, I'm matter-of-fact. I'm not reacting as I'm expected to react.

Other reactions puzzle me. As I walk down the street I pluck some leaves from a bush, crush and smush them in my hand. Immediately I feel an overwhelming sense of wrongdoing. The growing green leaves aren't for me to kill. The green leaves are . . . are what? The leaves are God's creation. I mustn't destroy them. Why am I thinking like this? What nonsense . . . people kill each other all the time . . . horribly . . . and I'm thinking of leaves? But no, no . . . I know that I don't think anymore of God as personal, but the world of sky, water, trees, flowers, bushes, birds and winds is God's world, nevertheless. That world, without people, is so beautiful; beautiful to see, smell, hear, and think about.

19

THE LAB SCHOOL

I walk three blocks, take the streetcar going east toward Lake Michigan, get off and walk north from 63rd Street to 59th Street, crossing a big open park area known as the "midway." From the first day I love the "school" part of the Lab School, also known as U-High. Teachers teach and in this school the thinking, learning life exists. For the next two years I'll love Mr. Edgett's social science class. He suggests that wars and social upheavals may have a historical (if not rational) explanation. I need to find an intellectually manageable idea to think about what has happened to me and my world in Europe. Passionate questions and convictions have their only outlet in his class. He requires us to outline the entire history book we use following each day's assignment. This awful task teaches me skills I won't appreciate until years later. He also is the ugliest man I've ever seen. This doesn't stop me having sexual fantasies about him. One morning he mentions in class that I'm to come with him to the principal's office. I try to think what I've done wrong. Scared, I come to the office to find out that a paper I wrote is the object of this visit. Mr. Edgett shows it to the principal, remarks on my recent acquaintance with English, and praises style and content. Now I glow a little inside. But I don't like that I automatically think I've done something wrong, I automatically think I'm in trouble.

In English class the teacher has the flexibility to assign me an alternate task after I shyly tell her I can't write an autobiography. When I started to write I began to cry and was afraid I'd never be able to stop. I was so frightened and upset that Mama noticed and asked, "What's wrong?" Instead I can write a sketch about one of the "Y" friends. But

155

when I give a book report about Pearl Buck's *The Good Earth,* I have no trouble explaining to the classmates the terrible poverty, famine, and being used as a slave.

In Latin class my teacher gives me help after school. I have trouble with verb conjugations. What are verb tenses? She explains about past, present, and future. I look at her blankly, not understanding. She explains some more and then I recognize in her face a look of total, "I give up." She tells me I'll just catch on as the lessons continue. I know nothing of past, present, or future time in English or Dutch, let alone Latin. Neither she nor I understand that the conjunction of an intellectual construct with an individual meaning about "time" prevents my learning. A sense of time is not a useable, knowable organizer within my head. In Latin class I suddenly think, "Would I know who I am if I didn't speak a language? What if I'd been left in the Russian zone and now spoke German? What would I be like if I'd been left there? Who am I? Who am I if being me is such a chancy thing?" After class I ask a question about this but there is no answer from the Latin teacher.

The social part of U-High is fascinating and puzzling. It's not bad, it's just that I miss understanding much of what goes on around me. I'm aware of the easy acceptance and offers of friendship from the girls in the "central" group. Friendship just happens. I don't have to do anything. And I don't do what the other girls do. I don't wear lipstick because I think it's revolting. I only have a few clothes that I make sure I wash and iron. I have one pair of shoes. I bet a girl that at the end of the year my shoes will still look new. I know I'll win the bet because I polish my shoes and I've noticed that the American girls don't take care of their shoes so they look worn very quickly. I travel home on two streetcars with one friend who lives high up in a very large apartment building on Michigan Avenue. A maid opens the door, and when we have a snack I know for sure my friend lives in a rich family. Her icebox opens to show food on every shelf and a whole salami. I can have as much as I want, not a few slices for the week as at home. Fleetingly I realize how strange and interesting it is that I've visited a family so poor that there's not enough food and now visit a family that is really rich.

For two years I try but cannot catch on to the "joking" language that snaps, crackles, and pops among girls and among boys and girls on the way to and from classes. Just understanding the English words doesn't give me the entrée to this language. I want to understand and do it too because they laugh, quicksilver laughing I would give my right arm for. Another puzzlement is "committees" and how they work. I'm encouraged to join the "girls club" and a committee to plan a dance in the spring. With a teacher attending and advising, everyone gets a task. Mine is to be responsible for the electric set-up. Only at the dance do I understand this means stringing colored lights and setting up a sound system. In the planning meeting I sat numb, not even knowing what to ask in order to get help. I don't know how or who got the work done. Much later I'll understand the intent; to teach by experience what democratic principle is all about. But after the dance I'm left with the belief that knowing what to do in this new world is beyond my reach. After all, the lights went on as if by magic and magic cannot be mastered.

I've been told that if you are good in math, you'll be good in science. I love math and always catch on quickly but science class is a mystery to me. It's not a mystery to Dannio. He does so well that a few years from now he'll take the National Merit Scholarship test and be awarded a four-year scholarship: tuition and room and board. He does so well that eventually he will earn a doctorate and become a research scientist. But I, here in freshman physics and chemistry, understand little. I can learn by rote and do well enough, but not understanding, not being drawn in my imagination to the periodic table, to the demonstrations with iron filings, to setting up an electric circuit with a positive and negative pole, leaves me dissatisfied. What is it? Is it our science teacher who doesn't answer the questions of girls? Is it that I'm ignorant of what the other kids have learned in this school since kindergarten? Is it that there is a part of me that doesn't want to see or hear, to notice or know? For many years science will be the one area where I cannot learn.

At home I don't understand Mama or myself. In the first months at the Eggleston house Mama makes me feel proud of her because the children who meet her tell me how pretty she is and how she seems like a sister, not at all like a mother. But now I only see Mama's face of suffering. I look at Mama, I listen to her unhappy, wailing voice, and I feel terrible. I feel torn up inside, just as if my insides are a wet dishtowel that you twist and wring. I want to fix that awful look on her face; I want to make it better for her. I think about that every day, every moment. I want to fix that awful look I see on her face. At the very same moment I hate that look, I hate to see and to hear her unhappiness. I feel a wrenching despair. All this leaves me with no protection when she gets angry or complains.

One day I come home to find out Mama has thrown out three of my treasures. The first is a navy peacoat that belonged to an older brother of one of my "Y" friends, to be appreciated when I cross the midway where the Chicago wind in winter whistles colder than any I've experienced. The second are my wood, curved Dutch skates. The third is the sleeping bag I made myself that I was so proud of. The "Y" friends have real sleeping bags. I took an old featherbed that Mama brought from Europe and I stuffed it into a waterproof cover I bought at the army/navy store. Now with a little sewing I, too, have a perfect sleeping bag. I can't believe she threw everything out. I can't quite believe she, my mama, would go into my closet and take things to throw out just like that. I ask her why and she says she's "cleaning up." I'm hurt and angry but mostly I feel, what's the use of being angry with her . . . it doesn't change anything.

She seems able to be unhappy with me and with life in general so easily but I can say nothing. When feelings build up in me I rush out of the room, slam a door, and cry and cry. One weekend Mama forbids me to go to the "Y" the following week because she and Tante Lisel have planned an outing. I explain and explain that I have to go. It's the day of a big water show that I am a part of; I can't just not show up. I also don't believe I'll get through the week if I can't be with my friends. It seems fruitless to argue; she doesn't budge but gets more and more angry. I will go. No matter what, I'll go. I can't bear not to go. But at some point I start to cry and now I cry without stopping. When the crying stops for a few minutes and I think maybe I can pull myself together, it starts again and again and again. In my room the afternoon passes and the evening and I have no control. I cry and feel that I will disappear, all of me will disappear in grief. When I awaken on Sunday morning it starts again. This is so awful and so frightening that I think, "There, that will stop it . . . it's unbearable." But it doesn't stop. Not until evening when I go to sleep, exhausted, do I have a feeing that I can stop crying. For days as I go to school and do what is required I feel dazed and exhausted.

Months ago I thought of running away but reality always stopped me. Where can I go? What will I eat? If I steal food there's a chance the cops will catch me. I'm terrified of police noticing me. I'm terrified of any adult authority getting power over me. One reason I'm so scared of going crazy is that then I expect they'll lock me up somewhere. I never think of running away to the relatives. They are so far away and seem so unreal, lost in a long-ago memory. I also have no sense that anyone would help me. It doesn't occur to me. And after all, I'm warm, have enough to eat, so how is it that I feel so terrible?

The days at U-High are an antidote to the days at home. But even there, I sometimes have that "breaking apart" feeling. We are shown a movie about civil defense. In the dark I watch school children react to a siren by getting under their desks. I start to think, "How stupid can grownups be? Even here at U-High?" To think that that will keep you safe from bombing, especially the atom bomb! Idiots! The next thing I know is that I have run down a hallway, found an empty classroom, and hear myself moan and cry. A little part of me wishes someone would come and find me, would put an arm around me. But I hide this out-burst like I try to hide all of that part of me. Once, long ago at the "Y" as we sat ready for lunch together, Betty started saying the Hebrew prayer before meals. She knew this because she'd grown up with lots of Jewish kids in her neighborhood, Hyde Park. I felt a stab of pain shoot through me and then I thought, "Is she making fun of me? Is she teas-ing me?" Before I knew what I was doing I'd run down the hall into a dark room and hid myself in a corner behind some stored furniture. It was very dark. I wanted to stay there and never, never come out again, never be with another human being ever again, never speak ever again. It took a long time and several people talking to me before I would come out. But I had no words to explain what had happened to me, no words at all.

In summer I'm able to go to the "Y" summer camp. I'll be a coun-selor-in-training. I get along well with the younger kids. I can teach, tell stories, lead them in singing, and with the girls in my tent I can be friends. With one of these friends I go to the nearest village on our day off. We get an ice cream and cross the street to the movie theater. In a surge of happy feeling I put my arm around her, an expression of friend-ship. She quickly throws off my arm and says sternly that I can't do that . . . people will think something bad. I'm not really clear about what would be bad but immediately feel terribly alone and a stranger again. In Holland my girlfriends and I would have walked arm-in-arm. Oh, America is hard! Still, when I'm dropped off at home at the end of the summer I stand on the porch, unwilling to open the front door to go in. I'd give anything not to have to go into that house.

U-High in 1950 is a two-year high school. At graduation in 1951 many of the kids will continue as early entrants to the University of Chicago. Some will finish at other four-year high schools. I am admitted to the University of Chicago and awarded an honor scholarship. I'll have to live at home and continue to commute to campus. When I cross the stage to receive my diploma, I say, "Thank you, oh, thank you for letting me come to U-High." Does the man handling out the diplomas have any idea what I'm talking about? Does he know what these two years have meant for me? I know that next September I will enter the U. of C. My relief at not having to go back to a Chicago high school is almost on the order of a death sentence reprieve. U-High is my adolescent oasis and U-High leads me to the University of Chicago.

20

UNIVERSITY OF CHICAGO

Freshman classes start in October, a few weeks after my sixteenth birthday. What do I know? I know I'm pretty enough for boys to ask me out. I know the "Y" friends told me I have a good figure. I know I didn't understand what they meant when they first told me. I know that I liked my breasts when they grew. They seemed just right. Why I felt happy I don't know, but I did. I know that I've grown apart from the "Y" friends. Two of the girls are married, one has a first baby. One has moved away and one is working full-time. One is studying as I am; she says she'll become a lawyer. In any case, classes, studying, and commuting use up most hours of the day. Now I swim on campus instead of the "Y." I know that in my readings I miss about every seventh word but the work is manageable anyway. I had no idea that the university would be so exciting, so different from anything I've ever experienced. The classes are taught in seminars. The professors prod us to think by asking questions and asking where logical conclusions might lead. I'm too shy to speak up often but listening to the examples given, the arguments, the unanswerable questions, and the innate contradictions leave my head spinning. But this world of ideas and new knowledge opens my mind. My mind is opened and fed nectar, stroked into sweet joy.

The first-year math course gives me a glimpse into a system of thinking, a purely imaginary construct that I find both intriguing and practical. I learn that Mr. W., the instructor, is from Poland and lost his wife and two children in Auschwitz. One afternoon I tell him where I've come from and as we walk down the second-floor stairs he turns to me and says, "You should think of going on in math; work, work is the only answer." I know that he means that you can drown your thoughts and memories in work and that that is what he has done. I completely miss hearing the first part of his advice.

I'm intimidated by the professors. Not yet have I acquired the American ease with authority. I'm intimidated by the other students who seem to know much more than I, who seem to speak easily, who seem so much smarter. What I learn is how little I know and how much, my God, how much there is to learn.

At home Mama is not as thrilled as I am. She wants me to learn practical things like typing. I believe she would prefer me to go to work. I try to remember that at sixteen I'd be a junior in a regular high school if I wasn't attending the U of C. I wouldn't be working full-time yet. Without thinking in words I have some inkling that university life is helping me to stay sane. What I don't understand yet is how anxious Mama is and that she would like me to be independent as soon as possible. At the end of the freshman year I get a wonderful invitation from Uncle Walter and Aunt Rena. Would I like to come to the farm for the summer, help with the work in the house and in the fields? Uncle Walter will even pay me a few hundred dollars for the summer. Would I like to! I'll be gone all summer. This will turn out to be the very best time of all my growing-up years since coming to America.

EPILOGUE

The farm summer was truly a happy time. After that, several young men fell in love with me at the university. I was still too childlike to respond, emotionally or physically. I continued to commute during my second year at university and worked part-time as a receptionist at a dance studio located across campus on the south side of the midway. At the start of the third year, in 1953, I moved into a very large private house on campus owned by the parents of a U-High friend. They rented out many rooms and I arranged to do housework in exchange for a lowered rent of seven dollars per week. Now I was on my own. A confluence of public and private events brought me to the brink of breakdown. This was the time of Senator Joseph McCarthy and the House UnAmerican Activities Committee. Every day the Chicago papers headlined another accusation. The era of witchhunts, blackballing, loyalty oaths, and jail sentences began. To me it sounded like the beginning of fascism. Not yet really understanding the intricacies and checks and balances of the American political system, I became more and more frightened. At the same time I was coming to the end of my college years. In this crucial transition time, hard for most young adults, I had to make decisions: "What's next? Do I work? At what? Do I go to graduate school? In what field? How?" I also met my future husband in my third year and this time I was ripe for love. To all this I could bring the strengths of my childhood. But these weren't enough for adult tasks and decisions. All other energy and emotional potential for growing up had been diverted to survival, learning a new culture, holding on, and staying sane. Finally, driven by fear to the University of Chicago mental health clinic, I was referred to Michael Reese Hospital. There I talked with a psychiatry resident once a week for all of six weeks. Somehow I got patched together for the time being and continued my path to adulthood.

At that time I made some resolutions; I gave myself some guidelines. First, I would not complain nor seriously take to heart anything unpleasant or difficult as long as I had food, safety, and warmth. Secondly, I would never indulge in quarreling about unimportant matters. Nothing was worth that misery unless it was a matter of "life and liberty." And, most important, I decided that I would live a "normal" life. No matter what it would take I would study, find work, marry, and raise children as though nothing unusual or terrible had ever happened to me. I would be just like "other" people. I became a teacher and a therapist. I married and raised three children to adulthood.

No one has ever known how hard it has been. The entry price of immigration is to have a vast subcontinent break away from the land mass that is the self. The radical rupture turns every known memory into an estranged one. Further, as a child I did not know that the decades of the twentieth century spewed forth refugees from countries around the world and deposited these refugees in a wild mosaic worldwide. As a child I did not know the statistics of murder or the specifics of the executions of my people. For decades there was complete silence. And so I could not allow inner knowledge of what I had experienced and what I felt. The numbness and the shutting off or hiding deeply of my feelings made it possible to go on. It also ensured that I would lose, gradually, all sense of who I was.

After many years I found my way back to Judaism. To live the seasons of the year and the cycles of life in a Jewish way is my task and my joy. To celebrate daily life—to experience and express gratitude for ordinary life events—is a gift of my Jewish heritage.

We came to America, America the huge. I arrived an unwilling settler, aghast at the loss of everything I still loved—my friends, my language, my place: "Mokum my Amsterdam." My Holland whose air, light, and ever-moving sky I loved.

We came to America, America the hope. I found acceptance. My merits enabled me to make a good life. We came to America where the ideals of the Founding Fathers and the republic they imagined offered possibilities for new attachments. America whose best philosophies mesh with the Jewish ideals I had learned by age seven.

Both Holland, my birth country, and America, my life country, think of themselves as the New Jerusalem, "the city on the hill." That is the language that speaks to my heart.

EPILOGUE

BLESSED BE YOU, OH GOD, CREATOR OF THE UNIVERSE, WHO HAS GIVEN US LIFE, HAS SUSTAINTED US AND BROUGHT US TO THIS DAY.[1]

Suzanne to Dr. Cullinan: "You know the *really* horrible thing is that it could have been worse. I *know* of *how* it could have been worse."

Dr. Cullinan to Suzanne: "I don't see how it could have been worse and you not dead."

---

[1]Part of the Jewish prayer beginning holidays, Shabbat, and special occasions.

RECOMMENDED BIBLIOGRAPHY

These books will give the reader an enriched understanding of Holland, the occupation, and medieval attitudes toward and of Jewish communities.

Blumenthal, W. Michael. *The Invisible Wall*. Washington, D.C.: Counterpoint, 1998. A moving, beautiful book that presents the history of Jews in Germany from the 1600s to the end of World War II. Using his own family tree, the author writes the social history of the German Jewish community in flowing, easy-to-follow language.

Gies, Miep, with Alison Leslie Gold. *Anne Frank Remembered: The Story of the Woman Who Helped to Hide the Frank Family*. New York: Simon and Schuster, 1987. A superb account of what life was like under the occupation of Holland for Gentile as well as Jewish Dutch citizens.

Gordon, Noah. *The Jerusalem Diamond*. Historical threads plus a gripping, modern story.

———. *The Physician*. New York: Ballantine Books, 1986. Highly entertaining, informative novel. Includes sections about Jewish communities in scattered sites in Europe and the Middle East in the thirteenth century.

Greenberg, Joanne. *The King's Persons*. New York: Holt, Rinehart, and Winston, 1963. An engaging historical novel, love story, and widely informative description of a Jewish community in England in the fifteenth century. By the author of *I Never Promised You a Rose Garden*.

167

Moskin, Marietta L. *I Am Rosemarie.* New York: The John Day Company, 1972. A biographical account of a Jewish teenager in Amsterdam, Westerbork, and Bergen-Belsen.

Warmbrunn, Werner. *The Dutch under German Occupation, 1940–1945.* Stanford: Stanford University Press, 1963. A sober, factual description of the history of the occupation years. Excellent, detailed scholarship.